Formulas

Solving math problems can be easy if you know some common mathematical formulas. Study the formulas below and use this page as a reference as you work through this book.

Abbreviations
pi = π = 3.14   r = radius   w = width   d = diameter
l = length   h = height   b = base   ∠ = angle

Area
of a circle: πr^2

of a square: w^2

of a rectangle: lw

of a triangle: $\frac{1}{2}$ (bh)

Surface Area
of a cylinder: $2(\pi r^2) + 2(\pi rh)$

of a cube: $6w^2$

of a sphere: $4\pi r^2$

of a rectangular prism: $2(ab + ac + bc)$; a, b, and c are the lengths of the 3 sides

Volume
of a cube: w^3

of a cylinder: $\pi r^2 h$

of a rectangular prism: lwh

of a cone: $\frac{1}{3} \pi r^2 h$

of a pyramid: $\frac{1}{3}$ (bh)

of a sphere: $\frac{1}{3} \pi r^3$

Perimeter
of a circle: πd or 2πr

of a square: 4w

of a rectangle: $2(a + b)$

of a triangle: $a + b + c$

Circumference
When given the diameter of a circle: πd

When given the radius of a circle: 2πr

Pythagorean Theorem: $a^2 + b^2 = c^2$

Assessment Test

1. Find the volume and surface area for the solid below.

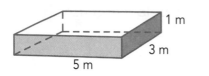

1 m

3 m

5 m

volume = _____

surface area = _____

2. The two legs of an isosceles trapezoid are congruent. Find the missing side lengths for isosceles trapezoid DEFG.

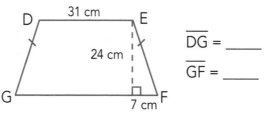

31 cm

24 cm

7 cm

$\overline{DG}$ = _____

$\overline{GF}$ = _____

3. Identify each of the following linear parts.

R   S   F   G   J   K

_____   _____   _____

4. Find the area and perimeter of the following triangle.

10 ft.

6 ft.

area = _____

perimeter = _____

5. Point D is the midpoint of CE. Find the values.

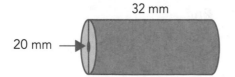

3x – 7   x + 11

C   D   E

x = _____   CD = _____   CE = _____

6. Find the volume and surface area of the cylinder below.

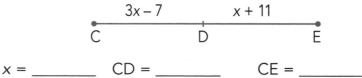

32 mm

20 mm

volume = _____

surface area = _____

7. Translate $\overline{AB}$ to the right 4 units and down 1 unit. Give the coordinates of the image points.

   A' (_____ , _____)

   B' (_____ , _____)

8. At 10:00 A.M., a 4-foot tall pole outdoors casts a 3-foot shadow. Determine the height of a building that casts a 60-foot shadow at the same time.

   _____

9. Find the missing angle measures. Then, classify each angle as acute, right, or obtuse.

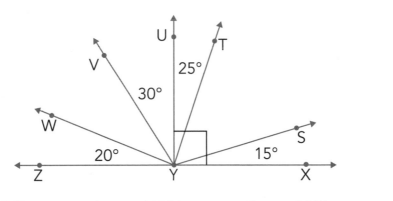

   m∠TYS = _____°   m∠WYV = _____°   m∠VYX = _____°

   _____   _____   _____

10. Find the sums of the measures of the interior angles for the following polygons. Use the formula $S = (n - 2) \cdot 180°$.

    hexagon = _____   octagon = _____

11. The interior angles of a quadrilateral equal 360°. Find the missing angle measures for quadrilateral GHIJ.

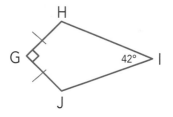

m∠H = _____ °

m∠J = _____ °

12. The interior angles of a triangle measure 180°. Find the missing angle measures.

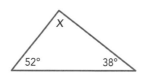

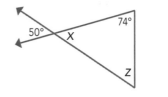

x = _____ °

x = _____ ° y = _____ °

13. Reflect ΔDEF over the x-axis. Give the coordinates of the reflected image points.

D' (_____ , _____)

E' (_____ , _____)

F' (_____ , _____)

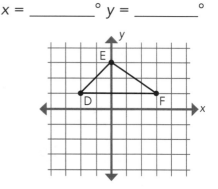

14. Draw the image that would be created after the given transformation.

translation right

180° rotation about point K

K

Check answers using the answer key provided (page 77). Match the problems with incorrect answers to the sections below. To ensure extra practice in problem areas, refer to the pages listed under each section.

Angles
Questions: 9, 11, 12
Review pages: 12–19

Pythagorean Theorem
Questions: 2, 4
Review pages: 32–34

Area
Question: 4
Review pages: 44–48

Quadrilaterals
Questions: 2, 11
Review pages: 35–37

Coordinate Geometry
Questions: 7, 13
Review pages: 69–76

Similarity
Question: 8
Review pages: 38–42

Linear Parts
Questions: 3, 5
Review pages: 8–11

Solids
Questions: 1, 6
Review pages: 53–65

Perimeter
Question: 4
Review pages: 43, 48

Transformations
Questions: 7, 13, 14
Review pages: 66–67

Pi
Question: 6
Review page: 50

Triangles
Questions: 4, 8, 12
Review pages: 25–34

Polygons
Question: 10
Review pages: 20–24

Lines

A **point** is a location in space. • A   Point A

A **line** is a set of points that extends infinitely in two directions. A ⟷ B $\overleftrightarrow{AB}$ or $\overleftrightarrow{BA}$

A **ray** is a part of a line with one endpoint. C D E → $\overrightarrow{DE}$ or $\overrightarrow{CE}$

A **segment** is a part of a line with two endpoints. F——G $\overline{FG}$ or $\overline{GF}$

A **plane** is a set of points that extends infinitely in two dimensions. H• •I •J   Plane HIJ

Identify and name each diagram.

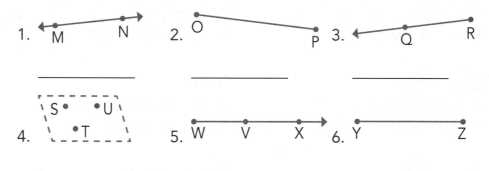

1. M N _____

2. O P _____

3. Q R _____

4. S• •U •T _____

5. W V X _____

6. Y Z _____

Draw and label each figure.

7. Plane ABC

8. $\overrightarrow{HI}$

9. $\overleftrightarrow{XY}$

10. ST

Linear Relationships

Colinear points lie in a line.

Parallel lines never intersect.

Perpendicular lines intersect at right angles.

Oblique lines intersect at non-right angles.

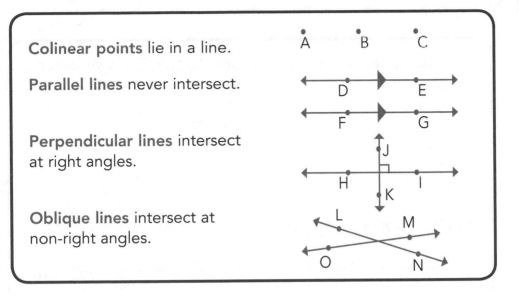

Use the diagram to name the following items.

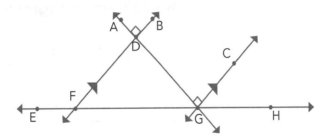

1. A pair of parallel lines

_____

2. A pair of oblique lines

_____

3. A pair of perpendicular lines

_____

4. Three colinear points

_____

5. Three non-colinear points

_____

6. Are two points always colinear?

_____

Congruent Segments and Segment Addition

Congruent segments have the same length. The symbol for *congruent* is ≅.

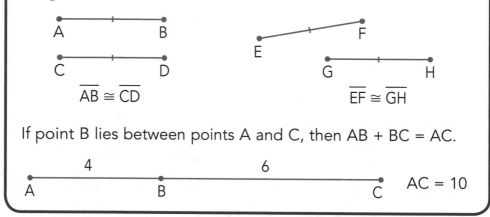

$\overline{AB} \cong \overline{CD}$

$\overline{EF} \cong \overline{GH}$

If point B lies between points A and C, then AB + BC = AC.

AC = 10

Find the length for each of the following segments.

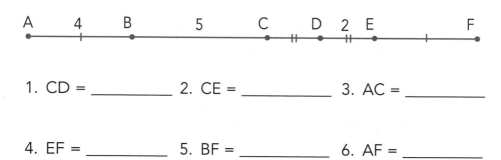

1. CD = _____

2. CE = _____

3. AC = _____

4. EF = _____

5. BF = _____

6. AF = _____

Using the number line, name a segment that is congruent to each given segment.

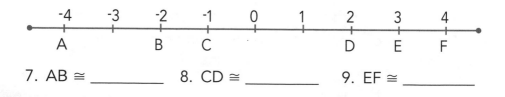

7. AB ≅ _____

8. CD ≅ _____

9. EF ≅ _____

Midpoints

A **midpoint** divides a segment into two congruent segments.

$\overline{AM} \cong \overline{MB}$

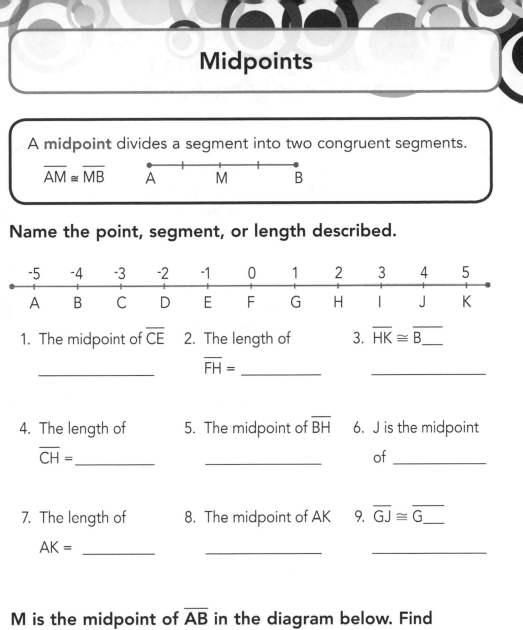

Name the point, segment, or length described.

-5	-4	-3	-2	-1	0	1	2	3	4	5
A	B	C	D	E	F	G	H	I	J	K

1. The midpoint of $\overline{CE}$

   _____

2. The length of

   $\overline{FH}$ = _____

3. $\overline{HK} \cong \overline{B\_\_}$

   _____

4. The length of

   $\overline{CH}$ = _____

5. The midpoint of $\overline{BH}$

   _____

6. J is the midpoint

   of _____

7. The length of

   AK = _____

8. The midpoint of AK

   _____

9. $\overline{GJ} \cong \overline{G\_\_}$

   _____

M is the midpoint of $\overline{AB}$ in the diagram below. Find these values.

4x – 10   x + 35

A   M   B

10. x = _____

11. AM = _____

12. AB = _____

Naming, Measuring, and Classifying Angles

An **angle** is formed by two rays with the same endpoint. An angle is named using three points. The **vertex**, or the point where the two rays intersect, must be the middle point.

∠ABC or ∠CBA

Acute angles measure between 0° and 90°, **right angles** measure exactly 90°, and **obtuse angles** measure between 90° and 180°.

Use a protractor to find the degree measure of each angle. Then, classify the angle as acute, right, or obtuse.

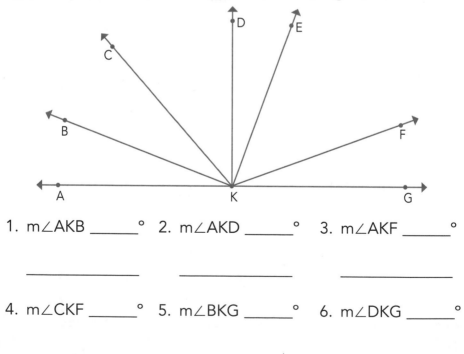

1. m∠AKB _____°

_____

2. m∠AKD _____°

_____

3. m∠AKF _____°

_____

4. m∠CKF _____°

_____

5. m∠BKG _____°

_____

6. m∠DKG _____°

_____

Congruent Angles and Angle Addition

Congruent angles have the same measure.

∠ABC ≅ ∠DEF

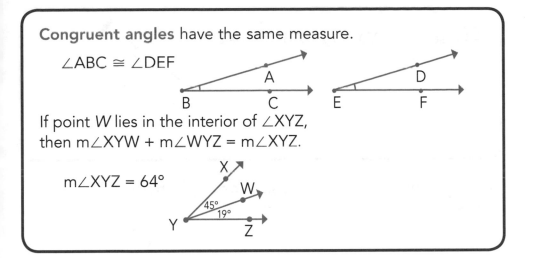

If point W lies in the interior of ∠XYZ,
then m∠XYW + m∠WYZ = m∠XYZ.

m∠XYZ = 64°

Find the angle measure or angle name.

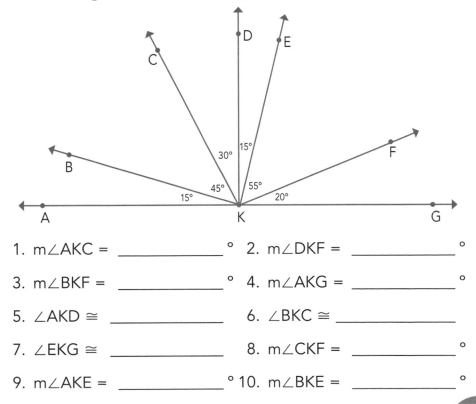

1. m∠AKC = _____° 2. m∠DKF = _____°

3. m∠BKF = _____° 4. m∠AKG = _____°

5. ∠AKD ≅ _____ 6. ∠BKC ≅ _____

7. ∠EKG ≅ _____ 8. m∠CKF = _____°

9. m∠AKE = _____° 10. m∠BKE = _____°

Angle Bisectors

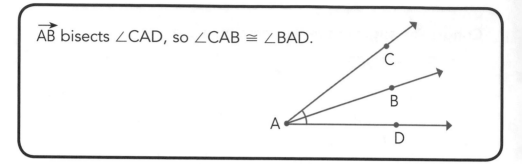

$\vec{AB}$ bisects $\angle CAD$, so $\angle CAB \cong \angle BAD$.

Find the missing angle measure or angle name. $\vec{BC}$, $\vec{NO}$, and $\vec{XY}$ are all angle bisectors.

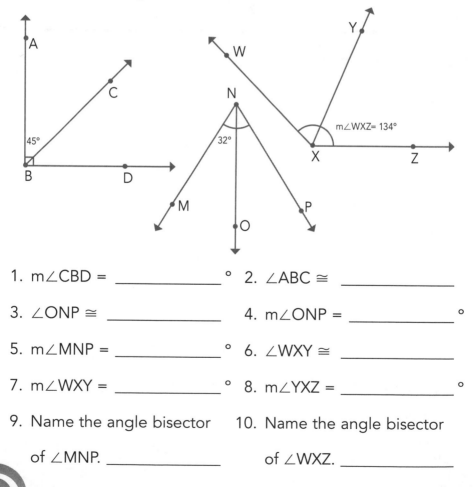

m∠WXZ= 134°

1. m∠CBD = _____°

2. ∠ABC ≅ _____

3. ∠ONP ≅ _____

4. m∠ONP = _____°

5. m∠MNP = _____°

6. ∠WXY ≅ _____

7. m∠WXY = _____°

8. m∠YXZ = _____°

9. Name the angle bisector of ∠MNP. _____

10. Name the angle bisector of ∠WXZ. _____

Complementary and Supplementary Angles

Complementary angles are two angles that add up to 90°.
Supplementary angles are two angles that add up to 180°.

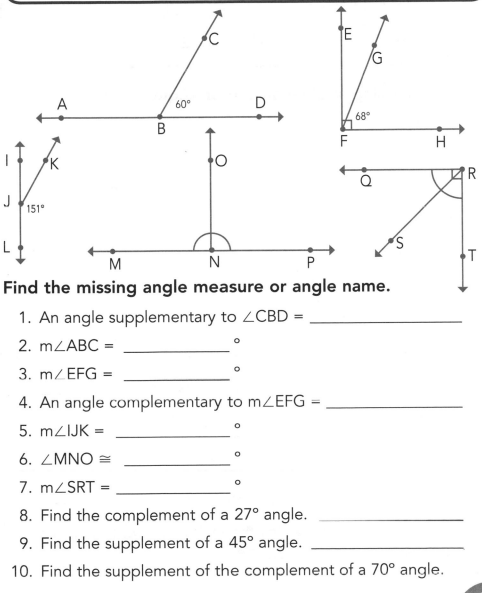

Find the missing angle measure or angle name.

1. An angle supplementary to ∠CBD = _____

2. m∠ABC = _____ °

3. m∠EFG = _____ °

4. An angle complementary to m∠EFG = _____

5. m∠IJK = _____ °

6. ∠MNO ≅ _____ °

7. m∠SRT = _____ °

8. Find the complement of a 27° angle. _____

9. Find the supplement of a 45° angle. _____

10. Find the supplement of the complement of a 70° angle.

_____

Vertical Angles

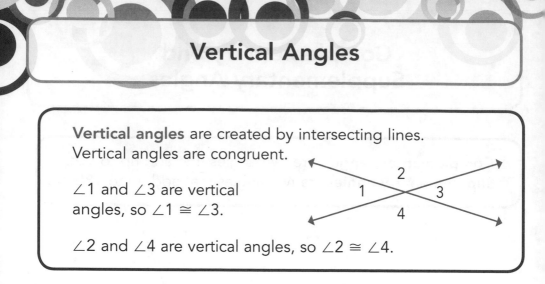

Vertical angles are created by intersecting lines. Vertical angles are congruent.

∠1 and ∠3 are vertical angles, so ∠1 ≅ ∠3.

∠2 and ∠4 are vertical angles, so ∠2 ≅ ∠4.

Find the missing angle measure or angle name.

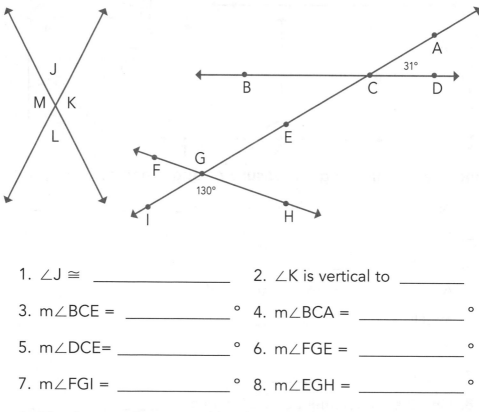

1. ∠J ≅ _____

2. ∠K is vertical to _____

3. m∠BCE = _____°

4. m∠BCA = _____°

5. m∠DCE= _____°

6. m∠FGE = _____°

7. m∠FGI = _____°

8. m∠EGH = _____°

9. The four angles created by the intersection of two lines will always equal _____ degrees.

Corresponding Angles

Corresponding angles are formed when a transversal (line) intersects two or more parallel lines. In the diagram, line T intersects lines M and N. The intersections form eight angles.

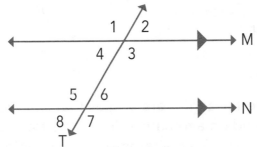

Corresponding angles are angles that sit in the same position at each intersection. For example, ∠1 and ∠5 are corresponding angles because both angles sit in the upper left corner of each intersection.

Other corresponding angle pairs include: ∠2 and ∠6, ∠3 and ∠7, ∠4 and ∠8.

Corresponding Angles Postulate: If two parallel lines are intersected by a transversal, then the corresponding angles that are formed are congruent.

In the above diagram, ∠1 ≅ ∠5, ∠2 ≅ ∠6, ∠3 ≅ ∠7, ∠4 ≅ ∠8.

Solve for x in each diagram.

x

$54°$

$2x + 10$

$5x - 8$

1. x = _____

2. x = _____

Alternate Interior and Exterior Angles

Alternate interior and alternate exterior angles are formed when a transversal intersects two or more parallel lines. In the diagram, line T intersects lines M and N.

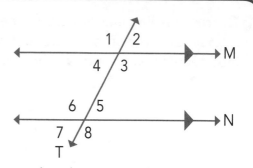

Alternate interior angles are angles that sit inside the parallel lines and on alternate sides of the transversal. For example, ∠3 and ∠6 are alternate interior angles.

Alternate exterior angles are angles that sit outside the parallel lines and on alternate sides of the transversal. For example, ∠1 and ∠8 are alternate exterior angles.

Alternate Interior Angles Theorem: If a transversal intersects two parallel lines, then the alternate interior angles are congruent.

Alternate Exterior Angles Theorem: If a transversal intersects two parallel lines, then the alternate exterior angles are congruent.

In the diagram, the following angles are congruent:
∠1 ≅ ∠8, ∠2 ≅ ∠7, ∠3 ≅ ∠6, ∠4 ≅ ∠5.

Solve for x, y, and z in the diagram.

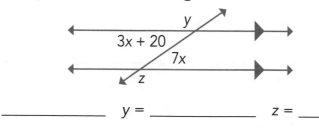

1. $x =$ _____ $y =$ _____ $z =$ _____

Same-Side Interior Angles

Same-side interior angles are formed when a transversal intersects two or more parallel lines. In the diagram, line T intersects lines M and N.

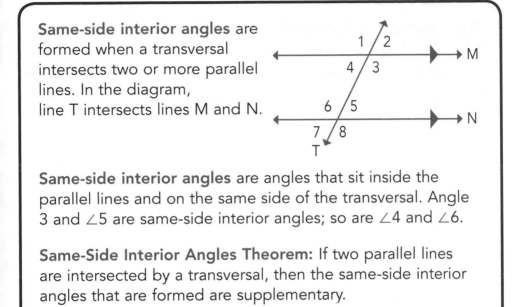

Same-side interior angles are angles that sit inside the parallel lines and on the same side of the transversal. Angle 3 and ∠5 are same-side interior angles; so are ∠4 and ∠6.

Same-Side Interior Angles Theorem: If two parallel lines are intersected by a transversal, then the same-side interior angles that are formed are supplementary.

In the diagram, $m\angle 3 + m\angle 5 = 180°$ and $m\angle 4 + m\angle 6 = 180°$.

Solve for x in each diagram.

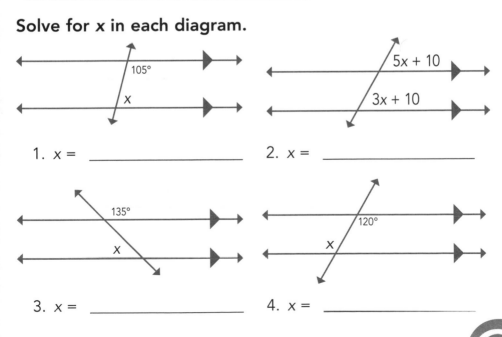

1. x = _____

2. x = _____

3. x = _____

4. x = _____

Classifying Polygons

A **polygon** is a closed figure made of segments that intersect only at endpoints.

1. Determine which figure(s) are polygons. Circle your answers.

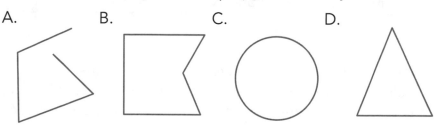

A.　　　　B.　　　　C.　　　　D.

Name each polygon according to the number of sides it has.

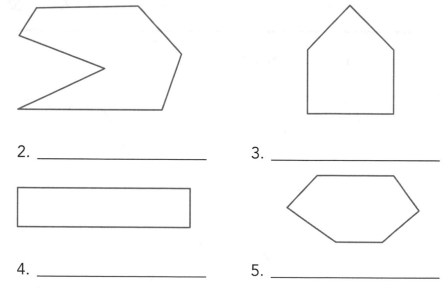

2. _____　　　3. _____

4. _____　　　5. _____

Polygon Angle Measures

The sum, *S*, of the measures of the interior angles of a polygon with *n* sides can be found by the formula $S = (n - 2) \cdot 180°$.

Find the sums of the measures of the interior angles for these polygons.

1. hexagon = _____

2. quadrilateral = _____

3. octagon = _____

4. heptagon = _____

5. pentagon = _____

6. triangle = _____

Find the measure of the angle marked x.

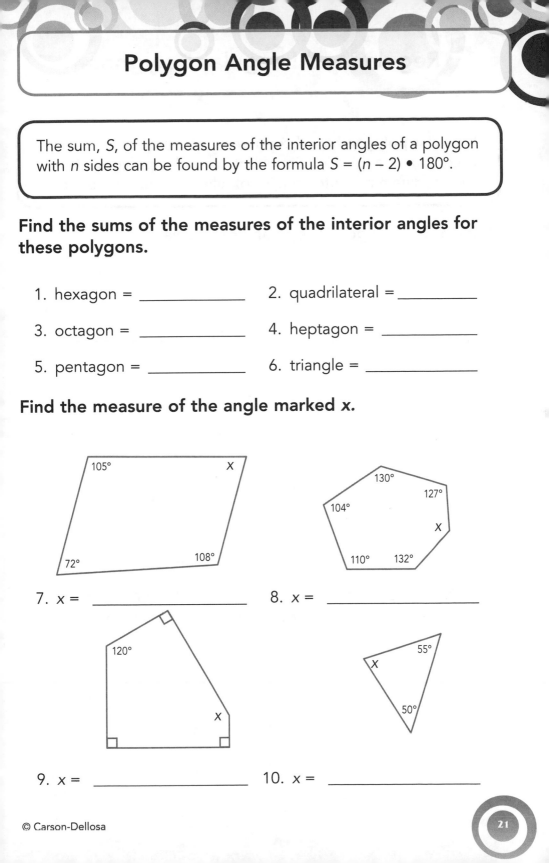

7. x = _____

8. x = _____

9. x = _____

10. x = _____

Regular and Irregular Polygons

A **regular polygon** has all congruent sides (**equilateral**) and all congruent angles (**equiangular**). **Irregular polygons** have sides of different lengths, angles of different measure, or both.

Write if the polygon is regular or irregular.

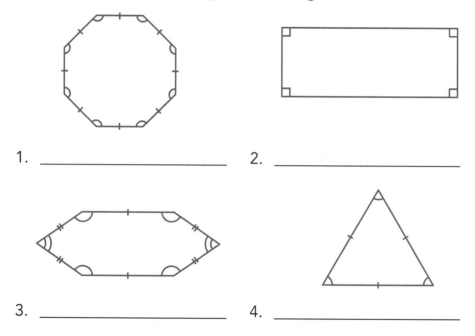

1. _____

2. _____

3. _____

4. _____

Find the measure of one interior angle for each regular polygon. Round answers to the nearest hundredth if necessary.

5. triangle = _____ °

6. quadrilateral = _____ °

7. pentagon = _____ °

8. hexagon = _____ °

9. heptagon = _____ °

10. octagon = _____ °

Drawing Polygons

A **convex polygon** has all angles pointing outward. The following polygons are examples of convex polygons.

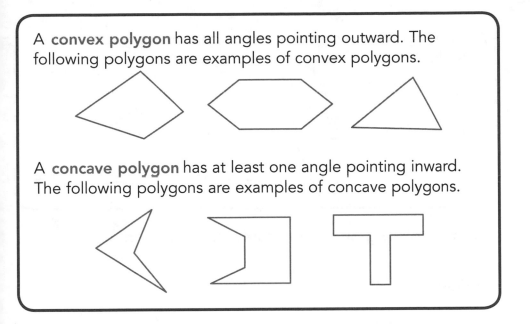

A **concave polygon** has at least one angle pointing inward. The following polygons are examples of concave polygons.

Draw each polygon.

1. an irregular pentagon

2. a regular hexagon

3. a convex quadrilateral

4. a concave quadrilateral

5. a regular octagon

6. an irregular octagon

Congruent Polygons

Two polygons are congruent if their corresponding side lengths and angle measures are congruent.

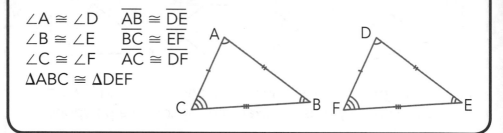

$\angle A \cong \angle D$ $\overline{AB} \cong \overline{DE}$
$\angle B \cong \angle E$ $\overline{BC} \cong \overline{EF}$
$\angle C \cong \angle F$ $\overline{AC} \cong \overline{DF}$
$\triangle ABC \cong \triangle DEF$

Find the missing angle measures or angle names.

pentagon ABCDE $\cong$ pentagon VWXYZ

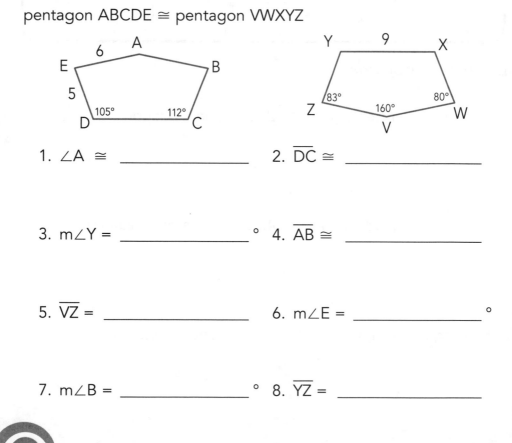

1. $\angle A \cong$ _____

2. $\overline{DC} \cong$ _____

3. $m\angle Y =$ _____ °

4. $\overline{AB} \cong$ _____

5. $\overline{VZ} =$ _____

6. $m\angle E =$ _____ °

7. $m\angle B =$ _____ °

8. $\overline{YZ} =$ _____

Classifying Triangles

Classifying by angle measures:

An **acute triangle** has three acute angles.

A **right triangle** has one right angle.

An **obtuse triangle** has one obtuse angle.

Classifying by side lengths:

A **scalene triangle** has no congruent sides.

An **isosceles triangle** has at least two congruent sides.

An **equilateral triangle** has three congruent sides.

Classify each triangle both by angle measures and side lengths.

1. _____

_____

2. _____

_____

3. _____

_____

4. _____

_____

5. _____

_____

6. _____

_____

Triangle Sum Theorem

The **interior angles** of a triangle equal 180°.

$m\angle A + m\angle B + m\angle C = 180°$

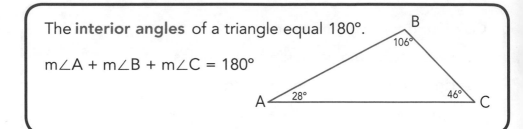

Find the missing angle measure for each triangle.

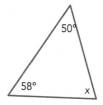

1. $m\angle x =$ _____ °   2. $m\angle x =$ _____ °

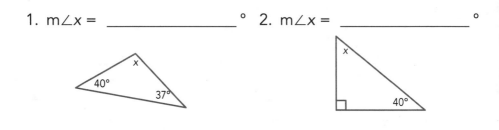

3. $m\angle x =$ _____ °   4. $m\angle x =$ _____ °

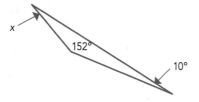

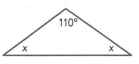

5. $m\angle x =$ _____ °   6. $m\angle x =$_____ °

Angle Measures of Triangles

The two base angles of an isosceles triangle are congruent.
All three angles of an equilateral triangle are congruent.

Find the missing measures in each triangle.

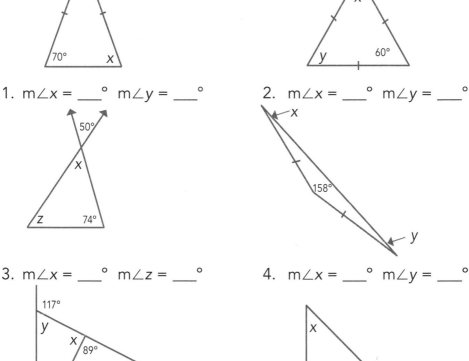

1. m∠x = ___° m∠y = ___°

2. m∠x = ___° m∠y = ___°

3. m∠x = ___° m∠z = ___°

4. m∠x = ___° m∠y = ___°

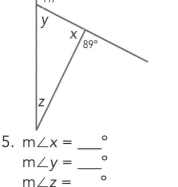

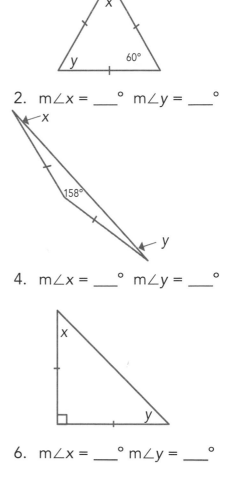

5. m∠x = ___°
   m∠y = ___°
   m∠z = ___°

6. m∠x = ___° m∠y = ___°

Angle Puzzle

Using the given information, fill in the measures of the rest of the angles in the diagram.

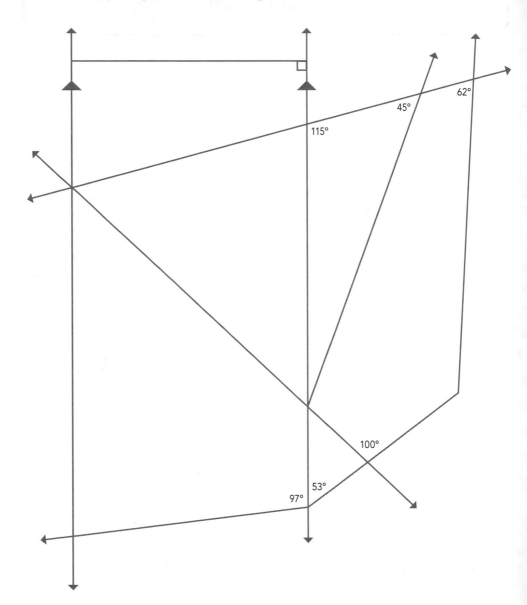

Congruent Triangles

Two triangles are congruent if:

- All three pairs of corresponding sides are congruent.
  Side Side Side (SSS)

- Two corresponding sides and the included angles are congruent. **Side Angle Side (SAS)**

Determine if each pair of triangles is congruent. If so, state the property that makes them congruent.

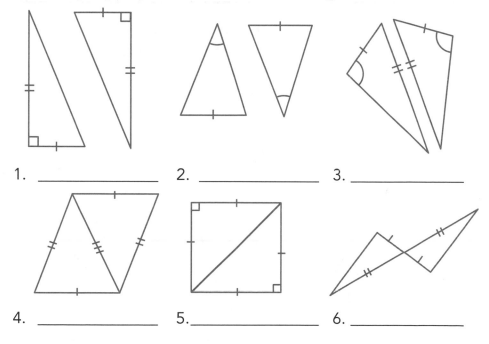

1. _____

2. _____

3. _____

4. _____

5. _____

6. _____

Congruent Triangles

Two triangles are congruent if:

- Two corresponding angles and the included side are congruent. **Angle Side Angle (ASA)**

- Two corresponding angles and a nonincluded side are congruent. **Angle Angle Side (AAS)**

- They are right triangles in which the hypotenuse and one leg of each triangle are congruent. **Hypotenuse Leg (HL)**

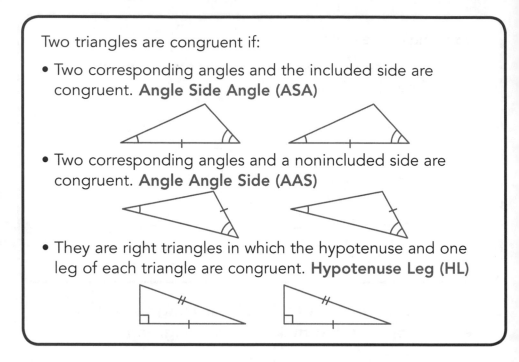

Determine if each pair of triangles is congruent. If so, state the property that makes them congruent.

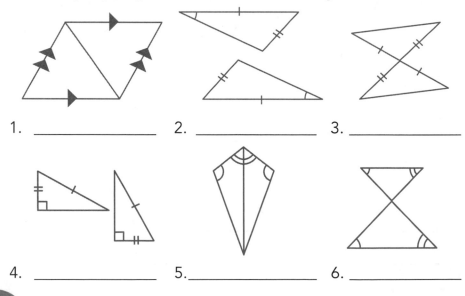

1. _____

2. _____

3. _____

4. _____

5. _____

6. _____

Parts of Congruent Triangles

Corresponding parts of congruent triangles are congruent.

$\angle A \cong \angle D$ $\overline{AB} \cong \overline{DE}$
$\angle B \cong \angle E$ $\overline{BC} \cong \overline{EF}$
$\angle C \cong \angle F$ $\overline{AC} \cong \overline{DF}$

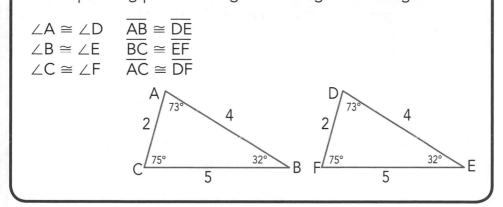

Find the missing measure for each pair of congruent triangles.

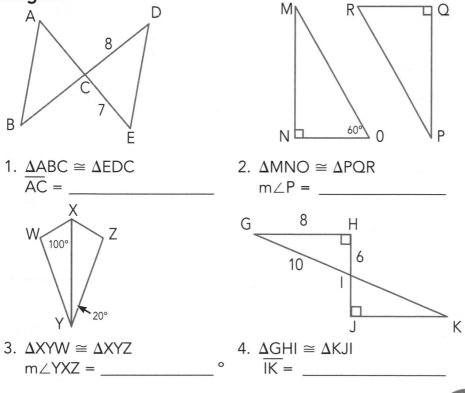

1. $\triangle ABC \cong \triangle EDC$
   $\overline{AC} =$ _____

2. $\triangle MNO \cong \triangle PQR$
   $m\angle P =$ _____

3. $\triangle XYW \cong \triangle XYZ$
   $m\angle YXZ =$ _____ °

4. $\triangle GHI \cong \triangle KJI$
   $\overline{IK} =$ _____

The Pythagorean Theorem

For a right triangle, the sum of the squares of the legs of the triangle equals the square of the hypotenuse. The **hypotenuse** is the side opposite the right angle.

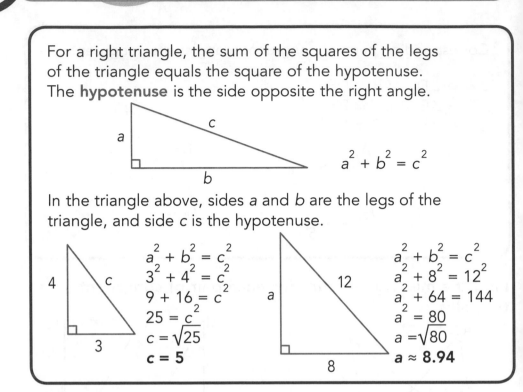

$$a^2 + b^2 = c^2$$

In the triangle above, sides a and b are the legs of the triangle, and side c is the hypotenuse.

$$a^2 + b^2 = c^2$$
$$3^2 + 4^2 = c^2$$
$$9 + 16 = c^2$$
$$25 = c^2$$
$$c = \sqrt{25}$$
$$\mathbf{c = 5}$$

$$a^2 + b^2 = c^2$$
$$a^2 + 8^2 = 12^2$$
$$a^2 + 64 = 144$$
$$a^2 = 80$$
$$a = \sqrt{80}$$
$$\mathbf{a \approx 8.94}$$

Find the missing side lengths. Round your answers to the nearest hundredth.

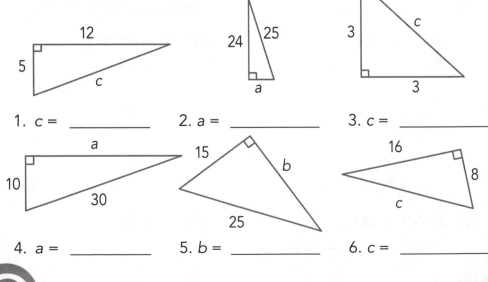

1. $c =$ _____   2. $a =$ _____   3. $c =$ _____

4. $a =$ _____   5. $b =$ _____   6. $c =$ _____

Applying the Pythagorean Theorem

Solve each problem. Round answers to the nearest hundredth.

1. A rectangle has side lengths of 8 cm and 11 cm. Find the length of the diagonal of the rectangle.

   _____

2. A square has a side length of 5 m. Find the length of the diagonal of the square.

   _____

3. A square has a diagonal with a length of 10 feet. Find the length of one side of the square.

   _____

4. A 40-foot-tall telephone pole is supported with a wire from the top of the pole to the ground. If the wire is attached to the ground at a spot 10 feet from the base of the pole, how long is the wire?

   _____

5. To get from home to school, Mischa must walk 0.75 miles east and 0.5 miles north. Determine the straight-line distance from Mischa's house to school.

   _____

The Converse of the Pythagorean Theorem

You can use the Pythagorean theorem to determine if a triangle is acute, right, or obtuse.

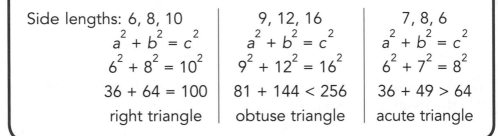

Side lengths: 6, 8, 10
$$a^2 + b^2 = c^2$$
$$6^2 + 8^2 = 10^2$$
$$36 + 64 = 100$$
right triangle

9, 12, 16
$$a^2 + b^2 = c^2$$
$$9^2 + 12^2 = 16^2$$
$$81 + 144 < 256$$
obtuse triangle

7, 8, 6
$$a^2 + b^2 = c^2$$
$$6^2 + 7^2 = 8^2$$
$$36 + 49 > 64$$
acute triangle

Determine if the three side lengths would make an acute, right, or obtuse triangle.

1. 3, 4, 5 _____

2. 5, 12, 11 _____

3. 20, 10, 12 _____

4. 0.7, 2.4, 2.5 _____

5. 5, 12, 13 _____

6. 6, 12, 8 _____

7. 6, 6, 11 _____

8. 5, 5, 5 _____

9. 9, 15, 12 _____

10. 50, 40, 30 _____

Classifying Quadrilaterals

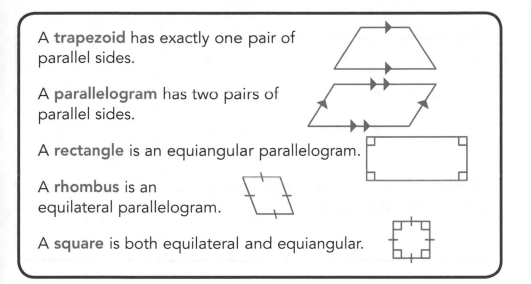

A **trapezoid** has exactly one pair of parallel sides.

A **parallelogram** has two pairs of parallel sides.

A **rectangle** is an equiangular parallelogram.

A **rhombus** is an equilateral parallelogram.

A **square** is both equilateral and equiangular.

Determine the type of each quadrilateral.

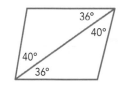

1. _____

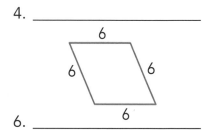

2. _____

3. _____

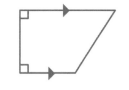

4. _____

5. _____

6. _____

Angle Measures of Quadrilaterals

The interior angles of a quadrilateral equal 360°.

$$58° + 130° + 47° + 125° = 360°$$

The opposite angles of a parallelogram are congruent.

The angles between the parallel sides of a trapezoid are supplementary.

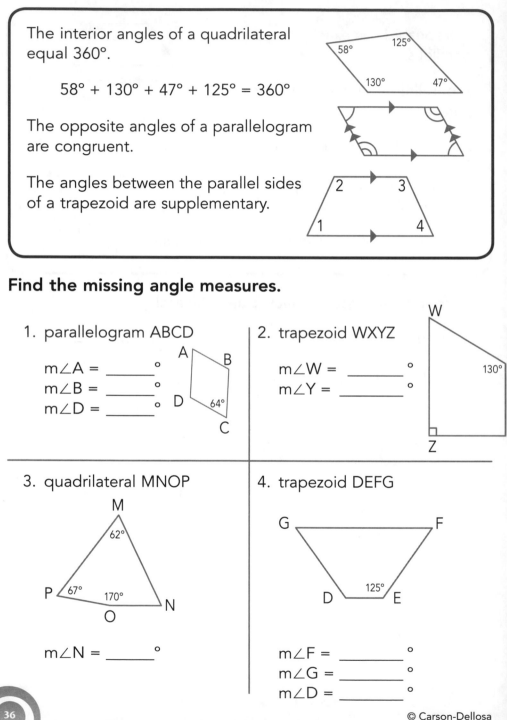

Find the missing angle measures.

1. parallelogram ABCD

   m∠A = _____°
   m∠B = _____°
   m∠D = _____°

2. trapezoid WXYZ

   m∠W = _____°
   m∠Y = _____°

3. quadrilateral MNOP

   m∠N = _____°

4. trapezoid DEFG

   m∠F = _____°
   m∠G = _____°
   m∠D = _____°

Side Lengths of Quadrilaterals

The opposite sides of a parallelogram are congruent.

All four sides of a rhombus are congruent.

The two legs of an isosceles trapezoid are congruent.

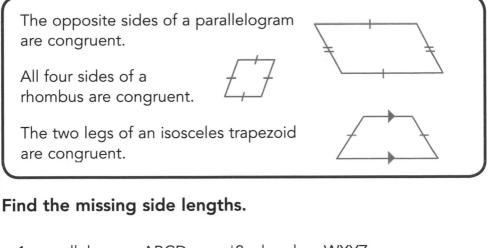

Find the missing side lengths.

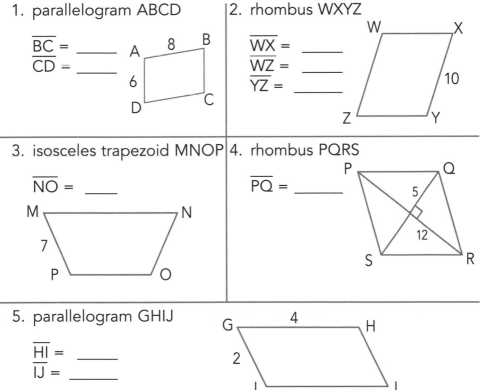

1. parallelogram ABCD

$\overline{BC}$ = _____
$\overline{CD}$ = _____

A   8   B

6

D   C

2. rhombus WXYZ

$\overline{WX}$ = _____
$\overline{WZ}$ = _____
$\overline{YZ}$ = _____

W   X

10

Z   Y

3. isosceles trapezoid MNOP

$\overline{NO}$ = _____

M   N

7

P   O

4. rhombus PQRS

$\overline{PQ}$ = _____

P   Q

5

12

S   R

5. parallelogram GHIJ

$\overline{HI}$ = _____
$\overline{IJ}$ = _____

G   4   H

2

J   I

Solving Proportions

A **proportion** shows that two ratios are equal.

To solve a proportion, cross multiply and solve.

$$\frac{10}{8} = \frac{y}{12}$$

$$10 \bullet 12 = 8 \bullet y$$
$$120 = 8y$$

$$y = 15$$

$$\frac{y}{7} = \frac{3}{5}$$

$$5y = 7 \bullet 3$$
$$5 \bullet y = 21$$

$$y = \frac{21}{5}$$

Solve for y.

1. $\frac{15}{y} = \frac{25}{5}$

   $y = \underline{\hspace{1cm}}$

2. $\frac{5}{7} = \frac{y}{21}$

   $y = \underline{\hspace{1cm}}$

3. $\frac{8}{14} = \frac{6}{y}$

   $y = \underline{\hspace{1cm}}$

4. $\frac{3}{13} = \frac{10}{y}$

   $y = \underline{\hspace{1cm}}$

5. $\frac{1}{6} = \frac{22}{y}$

   $y = \underline{\hspace{1cm}}$

6. $\frac{3}{5} = \frac{y}{35}$

   $y = \underline{\hspace{1cm}}$

Similar Polygons

Two polygons are **similar** if their corresponding angles are congruent and their corresponding side lengths are proportional.

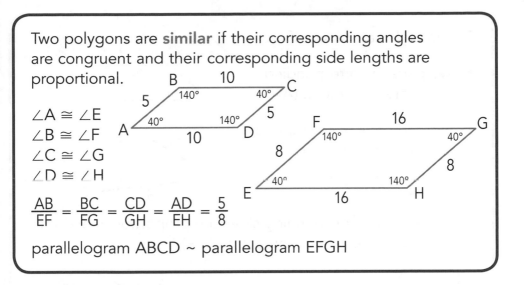

$\angle A \cong \angle E$
$\angle B \cong \angle F$
$\angle C \cong \angle G$
$\angle D \cong \angle H$

$\dfrac{AB}{EF} = \dfrac{BC}{FG} = \dfrac{CD}{GH} = \dfrac{AD}{EH} = \dfrac{5}{8}$

parallelogram ABCD ~ parallelogram EFGH

Determine if each pair of polygons is similar. Circle *yes* if the polygons are similar. Circle *no* if they are not.

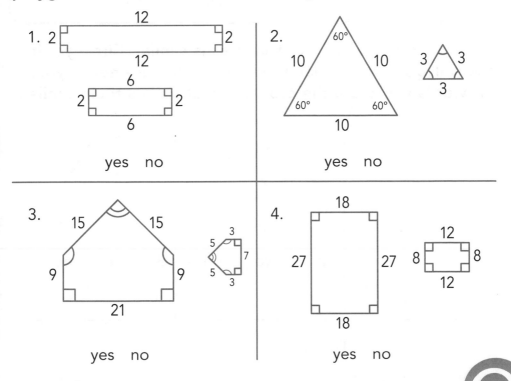

1. yes   no

2. yes   no

3. yes   no

4. yes   no

Similar Triangles

Two triangles are similar if:

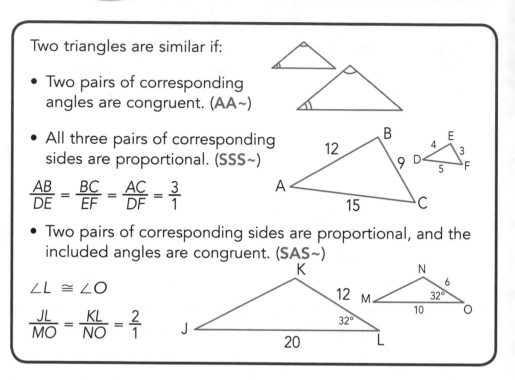

- Two pairs of corresponding angles are congruent. (**AA~**)

- All three pairs of corresponding sides are proportional. (**SSS~**)

$$\frac{AB}{DE} = \frac{BC}{EF} = \frac{AC}{DF} = \frac{3}{1}$$

- Two pairs of corresponding sides are proportional, and the included angles are congruent. (**SAS~**)

$$\angle L \cong \angle O$$

$$\frac{JL}{MO} = \frac{KL}{NO} = \frac{2}{1}$$

Determine if each pair of triangles is similar. Circle *yes* if the polygons are similar. Circle *no* if they are not. If your answer is yes, state the property that makes them similar.

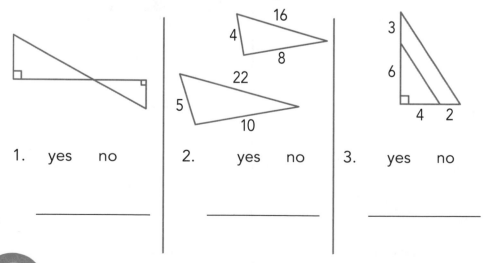

1.   yes   no

2.   yes   no

3.   yes   no

_____   _____   _____

Applying Similarity

If two polygons are similar, you can find missing side lengths or angle measures.

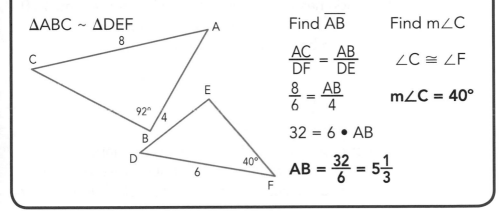

$\triangle ABC \sim \triangle DEF$

Find $\overline{AB}$

$$\frac{AC}{DF} = \frac{AB}{DE}$$

$$\frac{8}{6} = \frac{AB}{4}$$

$$32 = 6 \cdot AB$$

$$AB = \frac{32}{6} = 5\frac{1}{3}$$

Find $m\angle C$

$\angle C \cong \angle F$

$m\angle C = 40°$

Find the missing side lengths or angle measures.

pentagon JKLMN ~ pentagon VWXYZ

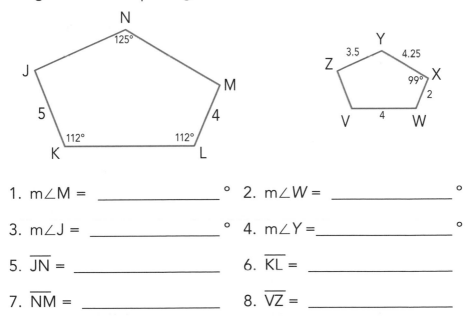

1. $m\angle M =$ _____°

2. $m\angle W =$ _____°

3. $m\angle J =$ _____°

4. $m\angle Y =$ _____°

5. $\overline{JN} =$ _____

6. $\overline{KL} =$ _____

7. $\overline{NM} =$ _____

8. $\overline{VZ} =$ _____

Applying Similarity

Use the properties of similar triangles to find each answer. Draw and label a sketch if necessary.

1. A map of Canada has a scale where 2 inches represents 250 miles. If you measure a distance of 7.5 inches on the map, determine the number of miles that represents.

   _____

2. If 1 centimeter represents 30 kilometers on a map, and Colorado is shown by a rectangle 20 centimeters long by 15 centimeters wide, calculate the area of Colorado in square kilometers.

   _____

3. If a map has a scale of 1 centimeter to 40 miles, and you take a 500-mile trip, determine how many centimeters this is on the map.

   _____

4. The blueprints of a rectangular room have a length of 7 inches and a width of 3 inches. If the actual room is built at a scale of 1 inch to 5 feet, determine the perimeter of the actual room.

   _____

Solving Perimeter Problems

The **perimeter** of a polygon is equal to the sum of all of the side lengths.

$$P = 10 + 7 + 10 + 7 = 34$$

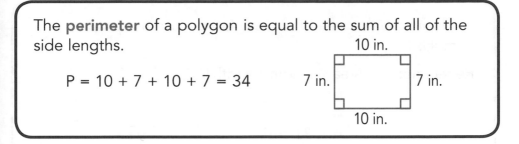

Find the perimeters of the following polygons.

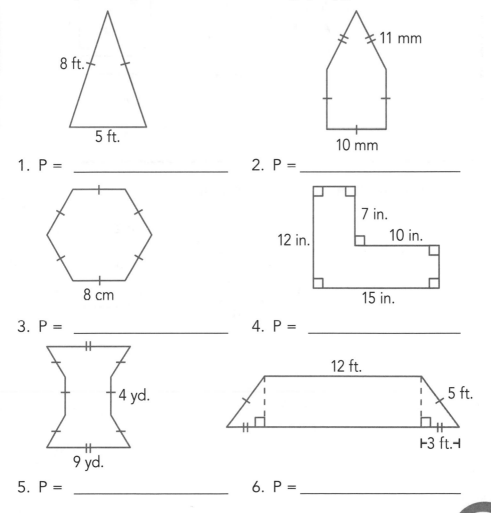

1. P = _____

2. P = _____

3. P = _____

4. P = _____

5. P = _____

6. P = _____

Area of Quadrilaterals

To determine the area of a quadrilateral, use the proper formula.

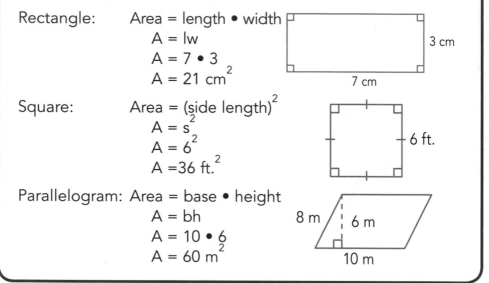

Rectangle:　　Area = length • width

$A = lw$

$A = 7 \cdot 3$

$A = 21 \text{ cm}^2$

3 cm

7 cm

Square:　　Area = (side length)^2

$A = s^2$

$A = 6^2$

$A = 36 \text{ ft.}^2$

6 ft.

Parallelogram:　Area = base • height

$A = bh$

$A = 10 \cdot 6$

$A = 60 \text{ m}^2$

8 m　6 m

10 m

Find the area of each quadrilateral.

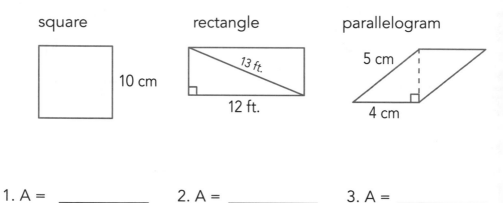

square

10 cm

rectangle

13 ft.

12 ft.

parallelogram

5 cm

4 cm

1. A = _____　　2. A = _____　　3. A = _____

Area of Triangles and Trapezoids

To determine the area of a triangle or trapezoid, use the proper formula.

Triangle: Area $= \frac{1}{2} \cdot$ base $\cdot$ height

$A = \frac{1}{2}$ bh

$A = \frac{1}{2}$ (10)(7)

$A = 35$ in.^{2}

Trapezoid: Area $= \frac{1}{2}$ (sum of the parallel bases) $\cdot$ height

$A = \frac{1}{2}$ $(b_1 + b_2)h$

$A = \frac{1}{2}$ (12 + 4)5

$A = 40$ in.^{2}

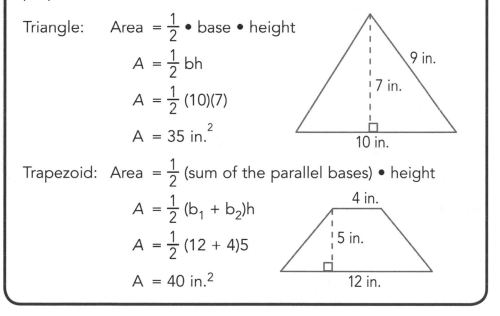

Find the area of each triangle or trapezoid.

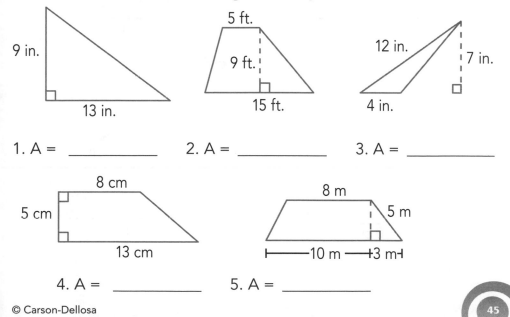

1. A = _____   2. A = _____   3. A = _____

4. A = _____   5. A = _____

Area of Irregular Shapes

To find the area of an irregular shape, divide it into known polygons.

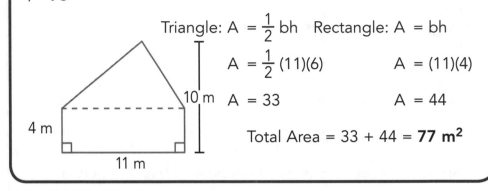

Triangle: $A = \frac{1}{2} bh$

$A = \frac{1}{2} (11)(6)$

$A = 33$

Rectangle: $A = bh$

$A = (11)(4)$

$A = 44$

Total Area = 33 + 44 = **77 m²**

10 m

4 m

11 m

Find the area of each irregular shape.

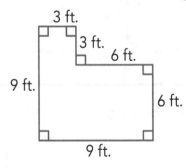

3 ft.

3 ft.

6 ft.

9 ft.

6 ft.

9 ft.

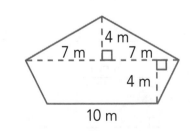

8 in.

25 in.

24 in.

15 in.

1. A = _____

2. A = _____

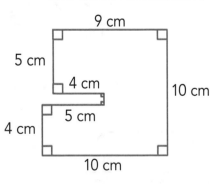

9 cm

5 cm

4 cm

10 cm

5 cm

4 cm

10 cm

4 m

7 m

7 m

4 m

10 m

3. A = _____

4. A = _____

Area of a Shaded Region

The area of a shaded region is equal to the total area of the shape minus the unshaded area.

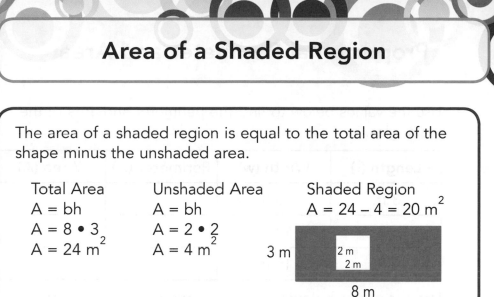

Total Area
$A = bh$
$A = 8 \cdot 3$
$A = 24 \text{ m}^2$

Unshaded Area
$A = bh$
$A = 2 \cdot 2$
$A = 4 \text{ m}^2$

Shaded Region
$A = 24 - 4 = 20 \text{ m}^2$

3 m

2 m
2 m

8 m

Find the area of each shaded region.

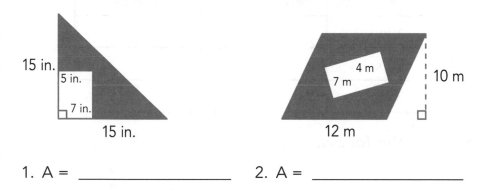

15 in.

5 in.

7 in.

15 in.

4 m
7 m

10 m

12 m

1. A = _____

2. A = _____

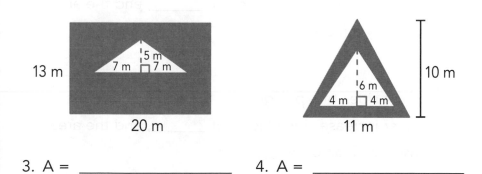

13 m

5 m
7 m   7 m

20 m

6 m
4 m   4 m

10 m

11 m

3. A = _____

4. A = _____

Proportional Perimeter and Area

1. Use the values below to find the perimeter and area of the rectangles.

Length (l)	Width (w)	Perimeter (P)	Area (A)
3 ft.	5 ft.		
6 ft.	10 ft.		
9 ft.	15 ft.		

2. Use the values below to find the perimeter and area of different-sized squares.

Side Length (s)	Perimeter (P)	Area (A)
1 in.		
2 in.		
3 in.		

Complete the following statements.

3. When the sides of a polygon are doubled in length, the perimeter increases by a factor of _____, and the area increases by a factor of _____.

4. When the sides of a polygon are tripled in length, the perimeter increases by a factor of _____, and the area increases by a factor of _____.

Parts of Circles

A **chord** is a segment whose endpoints lie on the circle.

The **diameter** is the longest chord of a circle; it passes through the center.

The **radius** of a circle is a segment from the center to the side of the circle.

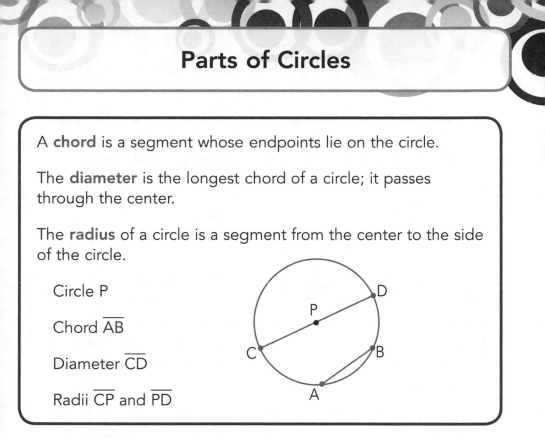

Circle P

Chord $\overline{AB}$

Diameter $\overline{CD}$

Radii $\overline{CP}$ and $\overline{PD}$

Give all possible answers for each circle part.

1. Chords _____

_____

2. Diameters _____

_____

3. Radii _____

_____

Tell whether each segment is a chord, diameter, radius, or none of these.

4. $\overline{AE}$ _____   5. $\overline{RD}$ _____

6. $\overline{BC}$ _____   7. $\overline{RA}$ _____

8. $\overline{BG}$ _____   9. $\overline{FH}$ _____

Discovering Pi

1. Measure the **circumference**, or the distance around a circle, by carefully wrapping a piece of string around each circle and then straightening it out and measuring it with a ruler.

2. Measure the diameter of each circle.

3. Enter both measurements in the table.

4. Divide the circumference by the diameter and write the answer in the last column.

Circle Number	Circumference (C)	Diameter (d)	C ÷ d
1			
2			
3			
4			
5			
6			

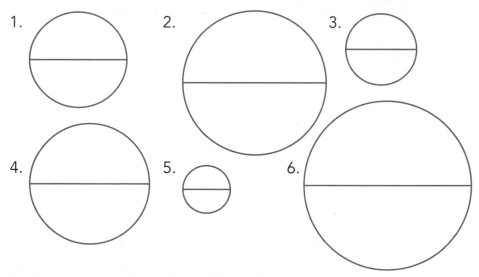

7. Find the average of the "C ÷ d" column entries. _____

8. **Pi (π)** is the ratio of circumference to diameter: 3.14
   Did your answer come close to 3.14? _____

Circumference

The **circumference** of a circle is the distance around the circle.

To determine the circumference of a circle, use one of two formulas:

Circumference = π • diameter   Circumference = 2 • π • radius

$$C = πd$$
$$C = (3.14)(12)$$
$$C = 37.68 \text{ in.}$$

12 in.

$$C = 2πr$$
$$C = 2 (3.14)(4)$$
$$C = 25.12 \text{ cm}$$

4 cm

Find the circumference of each circle.
Use π = 3.14.

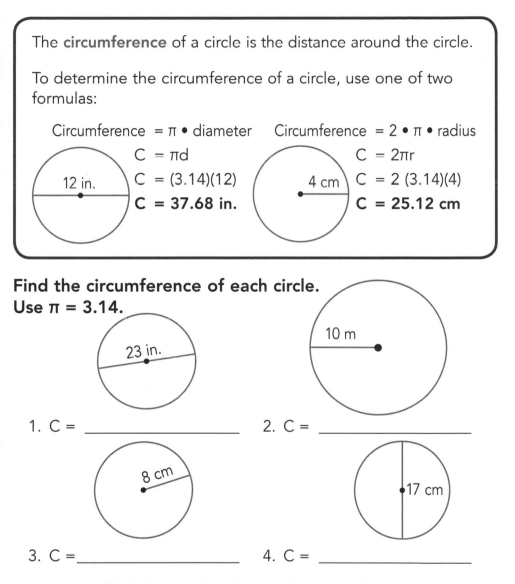

23 in.

10 m

1. C = _____

2. C = _____

8 cm

17 cm

3. C = _____

4. C = _____

5. A circle has a circumference of 62.8 in. Find the radius of the circle. _____

6. A circle has a circumference of 43.96 cm. Find the diameter of the circle. _____

Area of Circles

The **area** of a circle represents the amount of space in the interior of the circle.

To determine the area of a circle, use the formula:

$$A = \pi \bullet (radius)^2$$

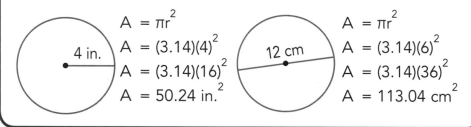

$$A = \pi r^2$$
$$A = (3.14)(4)^2$$
$$A = (3.14)(16)^2$$
$$A = 50.24 \text{ in.}^2$$

$$A = \pi r^2$$
$$A = (3.14)(6)^2$$
$$A = (3.14)(36)^2$$
$$A = 113.04 \text{ cm}^2$$

Find the area of each circle. Use π = 3.14.

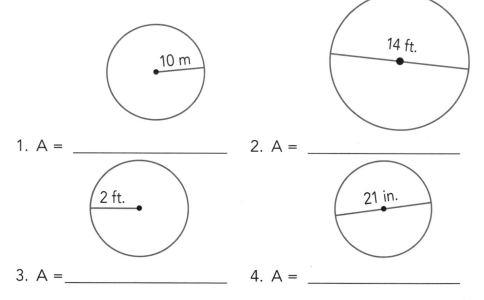

1. A = _____

2. A = _____

3. A = _____

4. A = _____

5. A circle has a diameter of 9.6 cm. Determine the area of the circle. _____

6. A circle has a circumference of 31.4 cm. Determine the area of the circle. _____

Classifying Solids

 A **prism** is a solid formed by two congruent polygon bases connected by rectangular lateral faces. A prism is named with regard to the polygon bases.

 A **cylinder** is a solid formed by two congruent circular bases and one curved side.

 A **pyramid** is a solid formed by one polygon base. The lateral faces are triangles that meet at a vertex. A pyramid is named with regard to the polygon base.

A **cone** is a solid formed by one circular base with a vertex at the opposite end.

Determine whether each given solid is a prism, cylinder, pyramid, or cone.

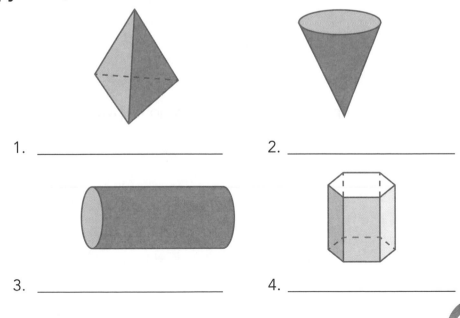

1. _____

2. _____

3. _____

4. _____

Drawing Solids

Draw each solid.

1. a rectangular prism

2. a cylinder

3. a triangular pyramid

4. a cone

5. a pentagonal prism

6. a pentagonal pyramid

Parts of a Prism

The **vertices** of a prism are the points of intersection.

The **edges** of a prism are the line segments that connect the vertices.

The **faces** of a prism are the planes that make up the sides.

A **cube** (rectangular prism) has 8 vertices, 12 edges, and 6 faces.

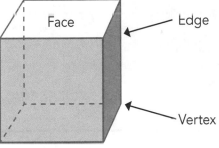

Fill in the following chart. Draw each prism if necessary.

	Type of Prism	Number of Vertices	Number of Edges	Number of Faces
1.	Triangular			
2.	Pentagonal			
3.	Hexagonal			
4.	Heptagonal			
5.	Octagonal			

6. Using your answers from the chart above, try to make predictions regarding the number of vertices, edges, and faces for any type of prism. If a prism has polygon bases with x number of sides, then the prism has:

_____ vertices, _____ edges, and _____ faces.

Viewing Solids from Different Perspectives

Solid objects can be viewed as two-dimensional objects from different perspectives.

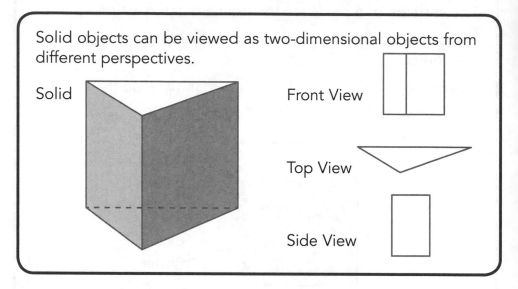

Solid

Front View

Top View

Side View

Draw the front view, top view, and side view for each solid.

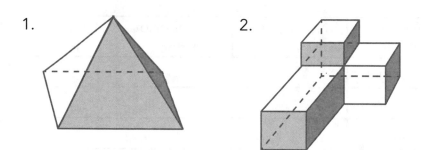

1.

2.

Viewing Solids from Different Perspectives

Solids can be drawn when given different perspective views.

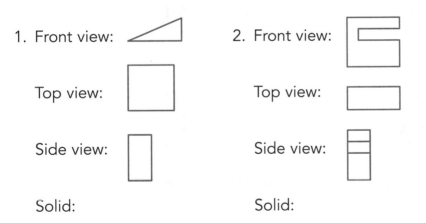

Draw the solids for the views given.

1. Front view:

   Top view:

   Side view:

   Solid:

2. Front view:

   Top view:

   Side view:

   Solid:

Nets

A **net** is a two-dimensional figure that represents an unfolded three-dimensional solid.

Solid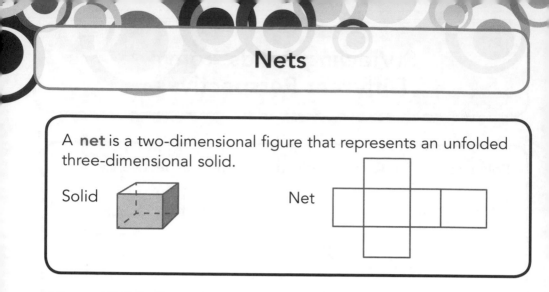

Net

When you draw a net, every face of the solid should be represented. Draw the net for each solid.

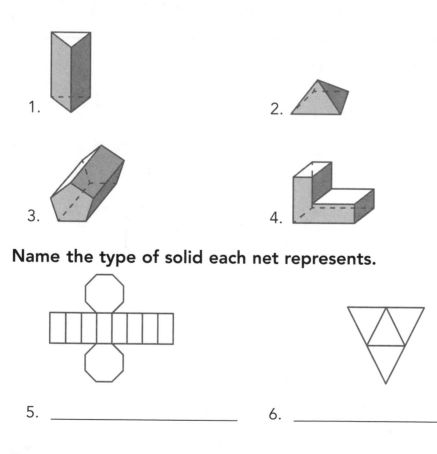

1.

2.

3.

4.

Name the type of solid each net represents.

5. _____

6. _____

Surface Area of a Prism

To find the **surface area of a prism:**

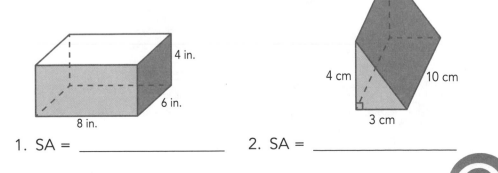

- Find the area of the lateral faces.
  Lateral Area = (**p**erimeter of one base) • (**h**eight of the prism)

  $L = ph$

  $L = (5 + 4 + 5) • 3$

  $L = 14 • 3 = 42 \text{ ft.}^2$

- Find the area of one base.
  Base Area = $\frac{1}{2}$ (length of one **b**ase) • (**h**eight of the prism)

  $B = \frac{1}{2} bh$

  $B - \frac{1}{2} (4)(3)$

  $B = 6 \text{ ft.}^2$

- Combine figures using the formula.
  Surface **A**rea = **L**ateral **A**rea + 2 (area of one base)

  $SA = L + 2B$

  $SA = 42 + 2 (6)$

  $SA = 54 \text{ ft.}^2$

Find the surface area of each prism.

1. SA = _____   2. SA = _____

Volume of a Prism

To find the **volume of a prism**, use the following formula:
Volume = (**B**ase area) • (**h**eight of the prism)

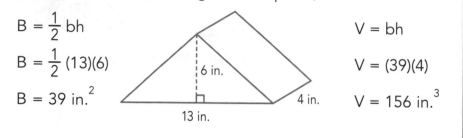

$B = \frac{1}{2} bh$

$B = \frac{1}{2} (13)(6)$

$B = 39$ in.^{2}

6 in.

13 in.

4 in.

$V = bh$

$V = (39)(4)$

$V = 156$ in.^{3}

Find the volume of each prism.

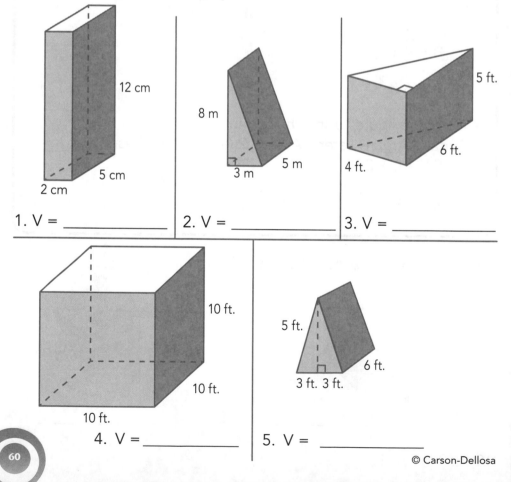

12 cm

5 cm

2 cm

8 m

3 m

5 m

5 ft.

6 ft.

4 ft.

1. V = _____

2. V = _____

3. V = _____

10 ft.

10 ft.

10 ft.

5 ft.

6 ft.

3 ft. 3 ft.

4. V = _____

5. V = _____

Surface Area of a Cylinder

The **height of a cylinder** is the distance between the two bases. To find the surface area of a cylinder, use the following formula:

Surface Area = 2 (area of the base) + (circumference of the base) × (height of the cylinder)

$SA = 2\pi r^2 + 2\pi rh$
$SA = 2\ (3.14)(2)^2 + 2\ (3.14)(2)(10)$
$SA = 150.72$ in.^{2}

Find the surface area of each cylinder. Use π = 3.14.

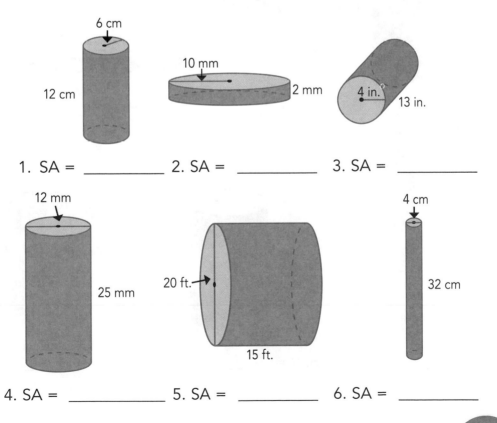

1. SA = _____

2. SA = _____

3. SA = _____

4. SA = _____

5. SA = _____

6. SA = _____

Volume of a Cylinder

To find the **volume of a cylinder**, use the following formula:

Volume = (area of the base) • (height of the cylinder)
$$V = \pi r^2 h$$
$$V = (3.14)(2)^2(10)$$
$$V = 125.6 \text{ in.}^3$$

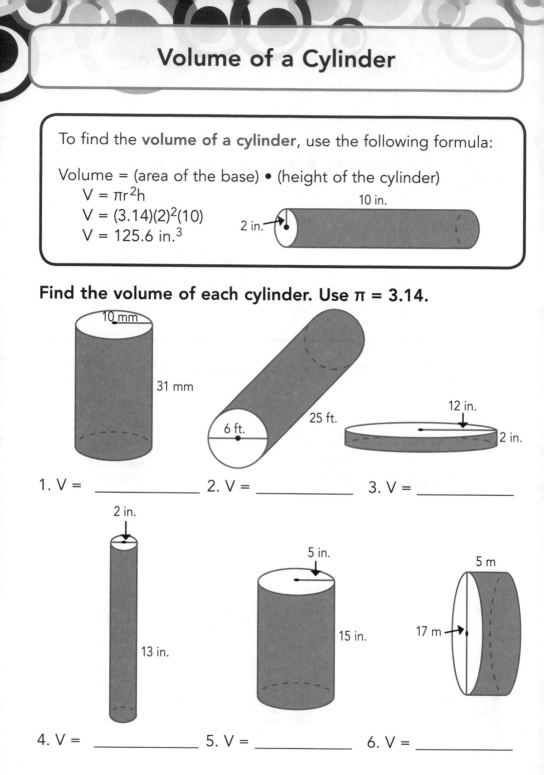

Find the volume of each cylinder. Use π = 3.14.

1. V = _____

2. V = _____

3. V = _____

4. V = _____

5. V = _____

6. V = _____

Surface Area Practice

Find the surface area of each solid. Use π = 3.14 when necessary.

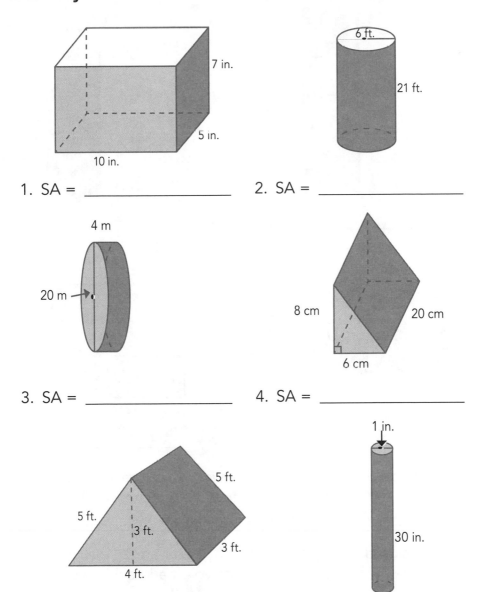

1. SA = _____

2. SA = _____

3. SA = _____

4. SA = _____

5. SA = _____

6. SA = _____

Volume Practice

Find the volume of each solid. Use π = 3.14 when necessary. Round your answers to the nearest hundredth.

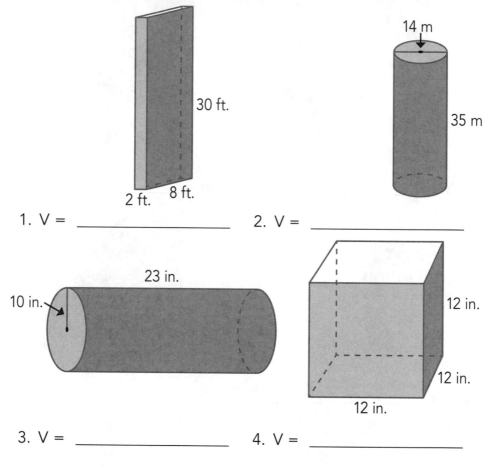

1. V = _____

2. V = _____

3. V = _____

4. V = _____

5. The inside dimensions of a microwave oven are 9 inches × 12 inches × 18 inches (1 cubic foot = 12 inches × 12 inches × 12 inches). What is its volume in cubic feet? _____

6. The inside dimensions of a chest freezer are 24 inches × 24 inches × 36 inches. What is its volume in cubic feet?

_____

Volume of a Sphere

To find the volume of a sphere, use the following formula:

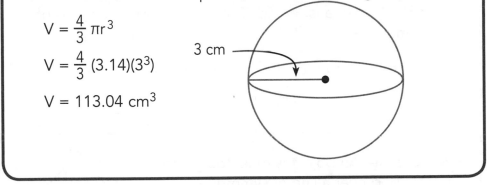

$V = \frac{4}{3} \pi r^3$

$V = \frac{4}{3} (3.14)(3^3)$

$V = 113.04$ cm^3

3 cm

Find the volume of each sphere with the given radius or diameter. Use π = 3.14. Round your answers to the nearest hundredth.

1. r = 5 in.

   V = _____

2. d = 14 ft.

   V = _____

3. d = 24 mi.

   V = _____

4. r = 10 cm

   V= _____

Identifying Transformations

The **image** of an object is the figure formed after the object has been transformed. There are four major types of transformations.

- **Translation**—An object is translated when it is moved in any direction.

- **Reflection**—An object is reflected when it is flipped over a line of symmetry.

- **Rotation**—An object is rotated when it is turned around a point.

- **Dilation**—An object is dilated when it is enlarged or reduced with respect to a point of dilation.

Name the type of transformation that created each image.

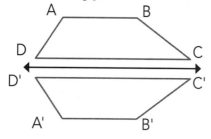

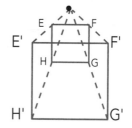

1. _____   2. _____

Drawing Transformations

Draw the image that would be created after the given transformation.

1. reflection

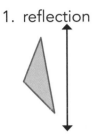

2. 180° rotation about point P

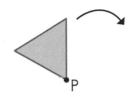

3. dilation from point P

4. translation to the right

5. 90° rotation about point P

6. translation down

7. reflection

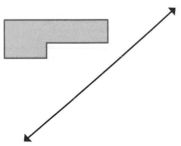

8. dilation from point P

Symmetry

When you draw a line through the center of a figure, and the two resulting figures are reflections of each other, then the figure has **reflectional symmetry**. A figure can have vertical reflectional symmetry, horizontal reflectional symmetry, or both.

When you rotate a figure about a central point, and the resulting image is congruent to the original figure, then the figure has **rotational symmetry**.

Determine whether each figure has reflectional symmetry, rotational symmetry, or neither.

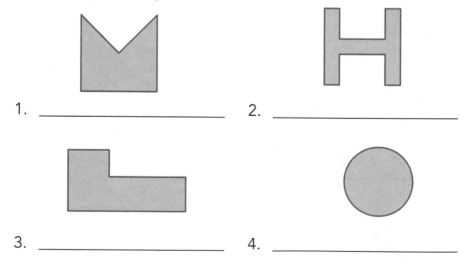

1. _____

2. _____

3. _____

4. _____

Identifying Points in a Coordinate Plane

Each point, except (0,0), in a coordinate plane is a result of two transformations: a horizontal translation (x-coordinate) and a vertical translation (y-coordinate) from the origin.

To describe the location of a point, use an ordered pair (x,y).

A (1,2)
right 1, up 2

B (-2,-1)
left 2, down 1

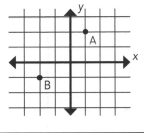

Give the ordered pair for each point on the graph.

1. A _____

2. B _____

3. C _____

4. D _____

5. E _____

6. F _____

7. G _____

8. H _____

9. I _____

10. J _____

11. K _____

12. L _____

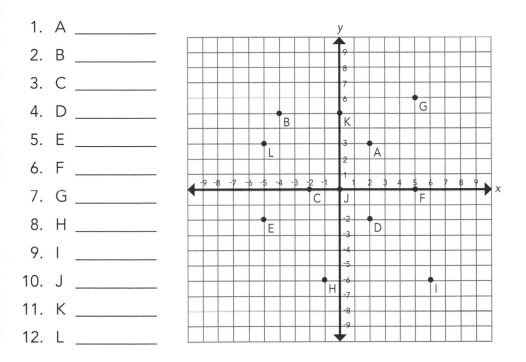

Plotting Points in a Coordinate Plane

Plot and label these ordered pairs as points on the coordinate plane.

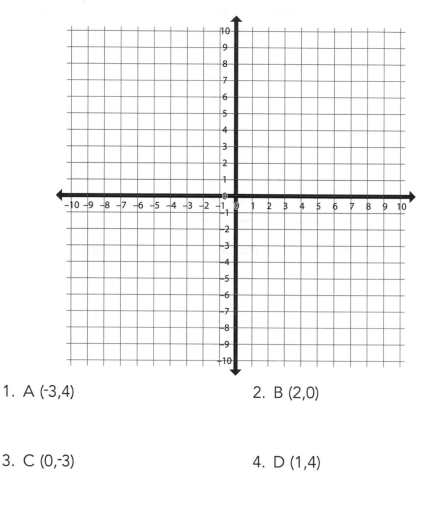

1. A (-3,4)

2. B (2,0)

3. C (0,-3)

4. D (1,4)

5. E (-3,-1)

6. F (2,2)

7. G (2,-2)

8. H (-1,-2)

Coordinate Translations

Each point of △ABC has been translated left 3 units and up 4 units. The image figure is labeled △A'B'C'.

A (1,0) → A' (1 – 3, 0 + 4) = A' (-2,4)
B (2,-3) → B' (2 – 3, -3 + 4) = B' (-1,1)
C (4,2) → C' (4 – 3, 2 + 4) = C' (1,6)

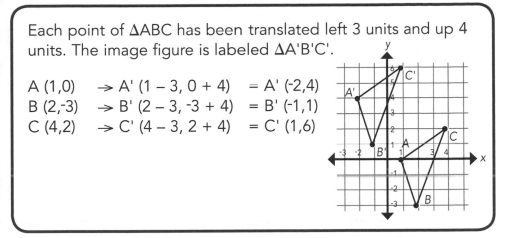

1. Translate △GHI to the left 1 unit and up 3 units. Give the coordinates of the image points.

   G' (_____ , _____)

   H' (_____ , _____)

   I' (_____ , _____)

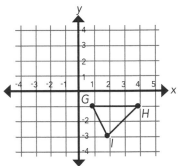

2. Translate rectangle WXYZ to the left 3 units. Give the coordinates of the image points.

   W' (_____ , _____)

   X' (_____ , _____)

   Y' (_____ , _____)

   Z' (_____ , _____)

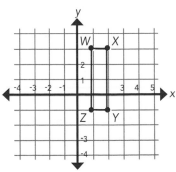

Coordinate Reflections

Each point of △ABC has been reflected over the x-axis.
The image figure is labeled △A'B'C'.

A (2,3) → A' (2,-3)
B (4,0) → B' (4,0)
C (1,4) → C' (1,-4)

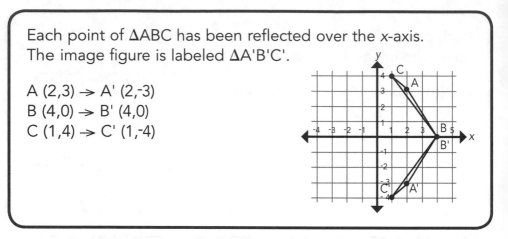

1. Reflect 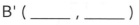 AB over the y-axis.
   Give the coordinates of the image points.

   A' (_____ , _____)

   B' (_____ , _____)

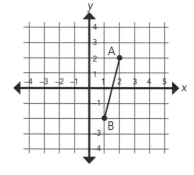

2. Reflect rectangle WXYZ over the x-axis.
   Give the coordinates of the image points.

   W' (_____ , _____)

   X' (_____ , _____)

   Y' (_____ , _____)

   Z' (_____ , _____)

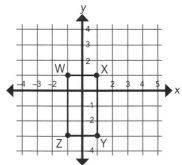

Coordinate Rotations

Each point of ΔABC has been rotated 90° clockwise around the **origin** (0,0). The image figure is labeled ΔA'B'C'.

A (-3,1) ➔ A' (1,3)
B (-2,4) ➔ B' (4,2)
C (-1,1) ➔ C' (1,1)

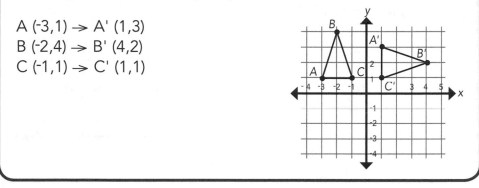

1. Rotate $\overline{AB}$ 180° clockwise around the origin.
    Give the coordinates of the image points.

    A' (_____ , _____)

    B' (_____ , _____)

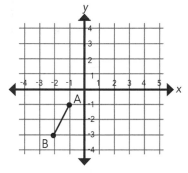

2. Rotate ΔDEF 90° clockwise around the origin.
    Give the coordinates of the image points.

    D' (_____ , _____)

    E' (_____ , _____)

    F' (_____ , _____)

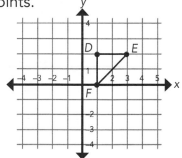

Coordinate Dilations

Each point of △ABC has been dilated from the origin. The image is twice as large as the original figure. The image figure is labeled △A'B'C'.

A (1,2) → A' (2,4)
B (3,3) → B' (6,6)
C (3,1) → C' (6,2)

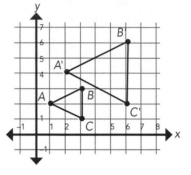

1. Dilate $\overline{AB}$ from the origin. Make the image three times as large as the original. Give the coordinates of the image points.

   A' (_____ , _____)

   B' (_____ , _____)

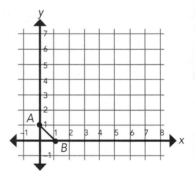

2. Dilate rectangle WXYZ from the origin. Make the image twice as large as the original. Give the coordinates of the image points.

   W' (_____ , _____)

   X' (_____ , _____)

   Y' (_____ , _____)

   Z' (_____ , _____)

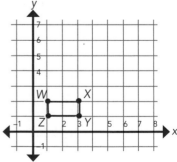

The Midpoint Formula

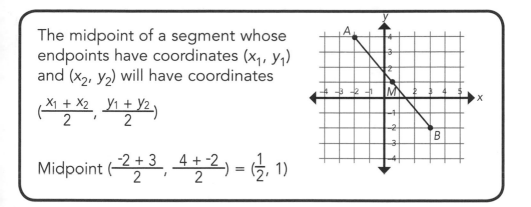

The midpoint of a segment whose endpoints have coordinates (x_1, y_1) and (x_2, y_2) will have coordinates

$$(\frac{x_1 + x_2}{2}, \frac{y_1 + y_2}{2})$$

Midpoint $(\frac{-2 + 3}{2}, \frac{4 + -2}{2}) = (\frac{1}{2}, 1)$

Given the coordinates for each set of endpoints, find the coordinates of the midpoint. Use the coordinate plane to draw each line segment and its midpoint.

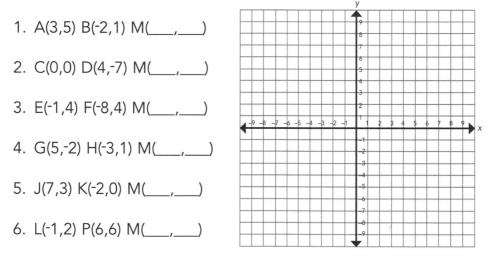

1. A(3,5) B(-2,1) M(___,___)

2. C(0,0) D(4,-7) M(___,___)

3. E(-1,4) F(-8,4) M(___,___)

4. G(5,-2) H(-3,1) M(___,___)

5. J(7,3) K(-2,0) M(___,___)

6. L(-1,2) P(6,6) M(___,___)

Given the coordinates for endpoint A and midpoint M, find the coordinates of endpoint B for each segment $\overline{AB}$.

7. A(3,2) M(4,4) B(___,___)

8. A(-2,-5) M(2,0) B(___,___)

The Distance Formula

The length of a segment whose endpoints have coordinates (x_1, y_1) and (x_2, y_2) can be found using the formula

$d^2 = (x_2 - x_1)^2 + (y_2 - y_1)^2$

$d = \sqrt{(x_2 - x_1)^2 + (y_2 - y_1)^2}$

$d = \sqrt{(3 - (\text{-}2))^2 + (\text{-}2 - 4)^2}$

$d = \sqrt{5^2 + (\text{-}6)^2}$

$d = \sqrt{25 + 36}$

$d = \sqrt{61}$

$\overline{AB} \approx 7.81$

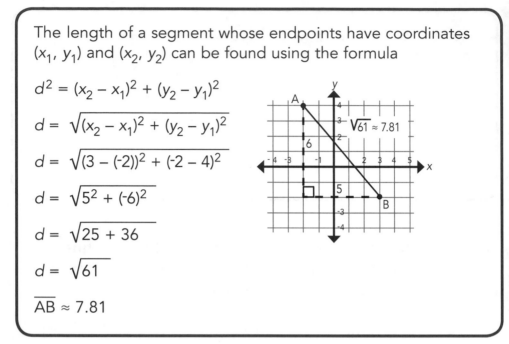

Given the coordinates for endpoints A and B, find the length of $\overline{AB}$. Round your answers to the nearest hundredth.

1. A(3,3)   B(-2,1) $\overline{AB}$ = _____

2. A(0,0)   B(4,-6) $\overline{AB}$ = _____

3. A(2,4)   B(-7,4) $\overline{AB}$ = _____

4. A(5,-2)   B(-2,1) $\overline{AB}$ = _____

5. A(7,3)   B(0,4) $\overline{AB}$ = _____

6. A(-1,2)   B(6,6) $\overline{AB}$ = _____

Answer Key

Pages 4–6
1. 15 m^3, 46 m; 2. 25 cm, 45 cm;
3. line, segment, ray; 4. 24 ft.^{2}, 24 ft.;
5. 9, 20, 40; 6. 10,048 mm^3, 2637.6 m^2;
7. A' = (2, 2), B' = (1, -1); 8. 80 ft.;
9. 50°, acute; 40°, acute; 120°, obtuse;
10. 720°, 1080°; 11. 114°, 114°; 12. 90°,
50°, 56°; 13. D' = (-2,-1), E' = (0,-3),
F' = (3,-1);

14.

Page 8
1. line, $\overleftrightarrow{MN}$ or $\overleftrightarrow{NM}$; 2. segment, $\overline{OP}$ or
$\overline{PO}$; 3. ray $\overrightarrow{RQ}$; 4. plane SUT; 5. ray,
$\overrightarrow{WX}$ or $\overrightarrow{WV}$; 6. segment $\overline{YZ}$ or $\overline{ZY}$;
7. ; 8. ; 9. ;
10.

Page 9
1. $\overleftrightarrow{BF} \parallel \overleftrightarrow{GC}$; 2. $\overleftrightarrow{EH}$ and $\overleftrightarrow{BF}$ or $\overleftrightarrow{GC}$;
3. $\overleftrightarrow{AG} \wedge \overleftrightarrow{BF}$ or $\overleftrightarrow{AG} \wedge \overleftrightarrow{GC}$; 4. B, D, F; E,
F, G, H; A, D, G; 5. any three points not
on the same line; 6. yes

Page 10
1. 2; 2. 4; 3. 9; 4. 4; 5. 13; 6. 17;
7. $\overline{DF}$; 8. $\overline{AC}$; 9. $\overline{BC}$ or $\overline{DE}$

Page 11
1. point D; 2. 2; 3. E; 4. 5; 5. E; 6. IK; 7. 10;
8. F; 9. D; 10. x = 15; 11. 50; 12. 100

Page 12
1. 20°, acute; 2. 90°, right; 3. 160°,
obtuse; 4. 113°, obtuse; 5. 159°, obtuse;
6. 90°, right

Page 13
1. 60°; 2. 70°; 3. 145°; 4. 180°;
5. ∠DKG or ∠BKE; 6. ∠CKE;
7. ∠BKD; 8. 100°; 9. 105°; 10. 90°

Page 14
1. 45°; 2. ∠CBD; 3. ∠MNO; 4. 32°;
5. 64°; 6. ∠YXZ; 7. 67°; 8. 67°;
9. $\overrightarrow{NO}$; 10. $\overrightarrow{XY}$

Page 15
1. ∠ABC; 2. 120°; 3. 22°; 4. ∠GFH; 5. 29°;
6. ∠ONP; 7. 45°; 8. 63°; 9. 135°; 10. 160°

Page 16
1. ∠L; 2. ∠M; 3. 31°; 4. 149°; 5. 149°;
6. 130°; 7. 50°; 8. 50°; 9. 360°

Page 17
1. x = 126°; 2. x = 6

Page 18
1. x = 5, y = 145°, z = 145°

Page 19
1. x = 75°; 2. x = 0; 3. x = 45°;
4. x = 120°

Page 20
1. B, D; 2. heptagon; 3. pentagon;
4. quadrilateral; 5. hexagon

Page 21
1. 720°; 2. 360°; 3. 1,080°; 4. 900°;
5. 540°; 6. 180°; 7. x = 75°;
8. x = 117°; 9. x = 150°; 10. x = 75°

Page 22
1. regular; 2. irregular; 3. irregular;
4. regular; 5. 60°; 6. 90°; 7. 108°;
8. 120°; 9. 128.57°; 10. 135°

Page 23
Answers for 1, 3, 4, and 6 will vary.
2. ; 5.

Page 24
1. ∠V; 2. $\overline{XY}$; 3. 105°; 4. $\overline{VW}$; 5. 6;
6. 83°; 7. 80°; 8. 5

Page 25
1. acute, equilateral; 2. obtuse, scalene;
3. acute, scalene; 4. right, isosceles;
5. acute, scalene; 6. obtuse, isosceles

Page 26
1. 51°; 2. 72°; 3. 103°; 4. 50° ; 5. 18°;
6. x = 35°

Page 27
1. x = 70°, y = 40°; 2. x = 60°, y = 60°;
3. x = 50°, z = 56°; 4. x = 11°, y = 11°;
5. x = 91°, y = 63°, z = 26°;
6. x = 45°, y = 45°

Answer Key

Page 28

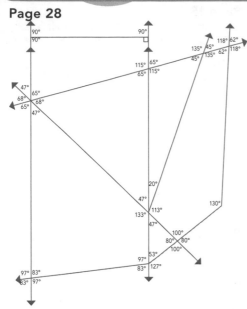

Page 29
1. yes, SAS; 2. no; 3. no; 4. yes, SSS;
5. yes, SAS or SSS; 6. yes, SAS

Page 30
1. yes, ASA; 2. no; 3. yes, SAS;
4. yes, HL; 5. yes, AAS; 6. no

Page 31
1. 8 ($\overline{EC}$); 2. 30°; 3. 60°; 4. 10 ($\overline{GI}$)

Page 32
1. $c = 13$; 2. $a = 7$; 3. $c = 4.24$;
4. $a = 28.28$; 5. $b = 20$; 6. $c = 17.89$

Page 33
1. 13.60 cm; 2. 7.07 m; 3. 7.07 ft.;
4. 41.23 ft. 5. 0.90 miles

Page 34
1. right; 2. acute; 3. obtuse; 4. right;
5. right; 6. obtuse; 7. obtuse; 8. acute;
9. right; 10. right

Page 35
1. parallelogram; 2. trapezoid; 3. square;
4. rectangle; 5. trapezoid; 6. rhombus

Page 36
1. m∠A = 64°, m∠B = 116°, m∠D = 116°;
2. m∠W = 50°, m∠Y = 90°; 3. m∠N = 61°;
4. m∠F = 55°, m∠G = 55°, m∠D = 125°

Page 37
1. $\overline{BC}$ = 6, $\overline{CD}$ = 8; 2. $\overline{WX}$ = $\overline{WZ}$ = $\overline{YZ}$ = 10;
3. $\overline{NO}$ = 7; 4. $\overline{PQ}$ = 13; 5. $\overline{HI}$ = 2, $\overline{IJ}$ = 4

Page 38
1. $y = 3$; 2. $y = 15$; 3. $y = 10.5$;
4. $y = \frac{130}{3} = 43\frac{1}{3}$; 5. $y = 132$; 6. $y = 21$

Page 39
1. no; 2. yes; 3. yes; 4. yes

Page 40
1. yes, AA~; 2. no; 3. yes, SAS~

Page 41
1. 99°; 2. 112°; 3. 92°; 4. 125°;
5. 7; 6. 8; 7. 8.5; 8. 2.5

Page 42
1. 937.5 miles; 2. 270,000 sq. km;
3. 12.5 cm; 4. 100 ft.

Page 43
1. 21 ft.; 2. 52 m; 3. 48 cm; 4. 54 in.;
5. 42 yd.; 6. 40 ft.

Page 44
1. 100 cm²; 2. 60 ft.²; 3. 12 cm²

Page 45
1. 58.5 in.²; 2. 90 ft.²; 3. 14 in.²;
4. 52.5 cm²; 5. 42 m²

Page 46
1. 63 ft.²; 2. 276 in.²; 3. 90 cm²; 4. 76 m²

Page 47
1. 77.5 in.²; 2. 92 m²; 3. 225 m²; 4. 31 m²

Page 48
1. Perimeter: 16 ft., 32 ft., 48 ft.; Area:
15 ft.², 60 ft.², 135 ft.²; 2. Perimeter: 4 in.,
8 in., 12 in.; Area: 1 in.², 4 in.², 9 in.²;
3. 2, 4; 4. 3, 9

Answer Key

Page 49
1. $\overline{AE}$, $\overline{BC}$, $\overline{EC}$, $\overline{DB}$, $\overline{EA}$, $\overline{CB}$, $\overline{CE}$, $\overline{BD}$;
2. $\overline{EC}$, $\overline{DB}$, $\overline{CE}$, $\overline{BD}$; 3. $\overline{XE}$, $\overline{XD}$, $\overline{XB}$
$\overline{XC}$, $\overline{EX}$, $\overline{DX}$, $\overline{BX}$, $\overline{CX}$; 4. diameter, chord;
5. radius; 6. none of these; 7. radius;
8. chord; 9. none of these

Page 50
Answers will vary, however every entry in the C ÷ d column should be approximately equal to 3.14.

Page 51
1. 72.22 in. 2. 62.8 m; 3. 50.24 cm;
4. 53.38 cm; 5. 10 in. 6. 14 cm

Page 52
1. 314 m^2; 2. 153.86 ft.^{2}; 3. 12.56 ft.^{2};
4. 346.19 in.^{2}; 5. 72.35 cm^2; 6. 78.5 cm^2

Page 53
1. triangular pyramid; 2. cone; 3. cylinder;
4. hexagonal prism

Page 54
Answers will vary.

Page 55
1. 6, 9, 5; 2. 10, 15, 7; 3. 12, 18, 8;
4. 14, 21, 9; 5. 16, 24, 10; 6. 2x, 3x, x + 2

Page 56
1. Front: 2. Front:

Side: Side:

Top: Top:

Page 57
1.   2.

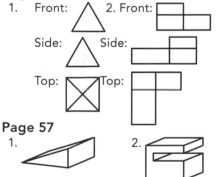

Page 58
1.   2.

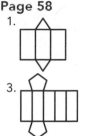

3.   4.

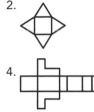

5. octagonal prism; 6. triangular pyramid

Page 59
1. 208 in.^{2}; 2. 132 cm^2

Page 60
1. 120 cm^3 ; 2. 60 m^3; 3. 60 ft.^{3};
4. 1,000 ft.^{3}; 5. 72 ft.^{3}

Page 61
1. 678.24 cm^2; 2. 753.6 mm^2;
3. 427.04 in.^{2}; 4. 1,168.08 mm^2;
5. 1,570 ft.^{2}; 6. 427.04 cm^2

Page 62
1. 9,734 mm^3; 2. 706.5 ft.^{3};
3. 904.32 in.^{3}; 4. 40.82 in.^{3};
5. 1,177.5 in.^{3}; 6. 1,134.33 m^3

Page 63
1. 310 in.^{2}; 2. 1,017.36 ft.^{2};
3. 879.2 m^2; 4. 528 cm^2;
5. 54 ft.^{2}; 6. 95.77 in.^{2}

Page 64
1. 480 ft.^{3} ; 2. 5,385.1 m^3;
3. 7,222 in.^{3}; 4. 1,728 in.^{3};
5. 1.125 ft.^{3}; 6. 12 ft.^{3}

Page 65
1. 523.33 in.^{3}; 2. 1,436.03 ft.^{3};
3. 7,234.56 mi.^{3}; 4. 4,186.67 cm^3

Page 66
1. reflection; 2. dilation

Answer Key

Page 67

1.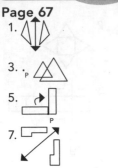

2.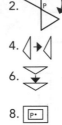

3.

4.

5.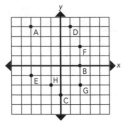

6.

7.

8.

Page 68

1. reflection; 2. reflection and rotation;
3. neither; 4. reflection and rotation

Page 69

1. (2, 3); 2. (-4, 5); 3. (-2, 0); 4. (2, -2);
5. (-5, -2); 6. (5, 0); 7. (5, 6); 8. (-1, -6);
9. (6, -6); 10. (0, 0); 11. (0, 5); 12. (-5, 3)

Page 70

1. through 8.

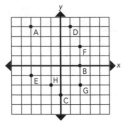

Page 71

1. G'(0, 2), H'(3, 2), I'(1, 0); 2. W'(-2, 3),
X'(-1, 3), Y'(-1, -1), Z'(-2, -1)

Page 72

1. A'(-2, 2), B'(-1, -2); 2. W'(-1, -1),
X'(1, -1), Y'(1, 3), Z'(-1, 3)

Page 73

1. A'(1, 1), B'(2, 3); 2. D'(2, -1), E'(2, -3),
F'(0, -1)

Page 74

1. A'(0, 3), B'(3, 0); 2. W'(2, 4), X'(6, 4),
Y'(6, 2), Z'(2, 2)

Page 75

1. $(\frac{1}{2}, 3)$; 2. $(2, -\frac{7}{2})$; 3. $(-\frac{9}{2}, 4)$; 4. $(1, -\frac{1}{2})$;
5. $(\frac{5}{2}, \frac{3}{2})$; 6. $(\frac{5}{2}, 4)$; 7. (5, 6); 8. (6, 5)

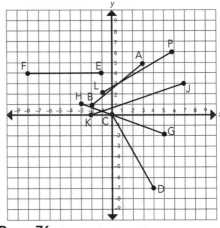

Page 76

1. 5.39; 2. 7.21; 3. 9; 4. 7.62; 5. 7.07;
6. 8.06